PLAB MEDICAL
MCQ PRACTICE PAPERS

Edited by

Simon A Allard BSc MBBS MD FRCP
Consultant Physician,
West Middlesex University Hospital.
Honorary Senior Lecturer,
Charing Cross and Westminster Medical School.

© 1995 PASTEST
Knutsford
Cheshire
Telephone: 01565 755226

First edition 1995

ISBN: 0 906896 67 3

A catalogue record for this book is available from the British Library.

Typeset by EDITEXT, Knutsford, Cheshire.
Printed by BPC Wheatons, Exeter.

CONTENTS

ACKNOWLEDGEMENTS

A sincere thank you is due to the following doctors whose contributions have made this book possible:

Dr Rashna Chenoy MRCOG, Senior Registrar/Lecturer, North Staffordshire Medical Centre, Stoke-on-Trent.

Dr Olivier A Harari MA MRCP, Registrar in Rheumatology and General Medicine, West Middlesex University Hospital.

Dr Gareth Holsgrove BEd MSc PhD, Senior Lecturer in Medical Education, St Bartholomew's and the Royal London Hospitals School of Medicine and Dentistry.

Mr David B Hocken MS FRCS, Consultant General and Vascular Surgeon, Princess Margaret Hospital, Swindon.

Dr Ian Maconochie MRCP, Research Fellow, St. Mary's Hospital, Paddington, London.

Mr Andrew Tapp MRCOG, Consultant, Department of Obstetrics and Gynaecology, The Royal Shrewsbury Hospital.

Special thanks also to Judith Wheeler at the British Council, Paul Walsh at the GMC, Dr Bogdan Nuta, Dr Mashkur Khan and Dr Carmen Munteanu.

FOREWORD

The multiple choice questions in this book are based on actual questions recalled by candidates from recent PLAB examinations. The scope of the subject matter covered reflects the common areas encountered in the medical MCQ section of the exam.

It is often said that the more one knows, the more difficult it is to answer MCQ questions. In some cases you may have to make a positive decision not to answer 'true' or 'false' (i.e. choosing the 'don't know' option) for questions that are ambiguous or unclear. This can be very frustrating in subject areas in which one feels confident.

Practice exams are a useful way of both testing your own knowledge base and evaluating your success rate at educated guessing. Research has shown that careful educated guessing almost always increases candidates' marks in MCQ papers, if the candidates' knowledge base is sufficient. It is worthwhile practising some of the tests with and without educated guessing to see if you are a 'good guesser'. If you are not (i.e. you score a lower mark with educated guessing), you may need to do more basic revision.

The introduction and hints on exam technique included in this book are provided as a guideline for practice revision.

I hope you enjoy practising with these questions and benefit from the explanations provided in the answer section. Don't forget to practise the exams before looking at the answers! Good luck on the day of your test.

Dr Simon Allard

v

GENERAL TIPS FOR PLAB CANDIDATES

1. Try to get a clinical attachment in the UK. The advantages are:

   - you will have a local reference
   - you will know the NHS system
   - the hospital may provide cheap accommodation
   - your English will improve and you will hear colloquial phrases
   - you will come across English illnesses

   In order to get a clinical attachment you will need to write to an individual Consultant or the hospital's Clinical Tutor enclosing your curriculum vitae (CV).

   A good CV must include details of what you have actually done (i.e. lumbar puncture, central line, sigmoidoscopy, putting in a chest drain). Just stating your medical school and length of time as an SHO is not enough to convince a Consultant that you are serious.

2. The Westminster Library on Marylebone High Street, London, is a large medical library that is particularly good for borrowing books.

3. The Royal College of Surgeons, 35–43 Lincoln's Inn Fields, London WC2A 3PN has specimens on display with detailed explanatory labels attached. This can provide some useful information for vivas.

4. If possible, form a study group with two other doctors to test yourselves in actual viva situations. Practise by having two doctors on one side of a table shooting questions at the third member of the group and set a clock for 20-minute sessions.

5. Listen to the radio or watch television, especially any medical programmes that are broadcast.

6. Read up on topical articles (e.g. *in vitro* fertilisation, post-coital contraception, abortion, euthanasia, care of the dying, bereavement, etc.).

7. You will initially be on a six-months' visitor's visa which can only be extended once. This means that you should waste no time in passing the PLAB. When you get a job you will be given a four-year permit free training visa.

INTRODUCTION

Overseas-qualified doctors wishing to come to the United Kingdom (UK) should be fully aware of the requirements both legal and professional before planning any visit to this country. Enquiries should be made about training in the UK before they consider contacting the General Medical Council (GMC) about the PLAB examination.

Those seeking assistance should contact the National Advice Centre for Postgraduate Medical Education (NACPME) at the British Council in Manchester which offers an information and advisory service for overseas-qualified doctors who wish to undertake medical training in the UK. Enquiries should be sent to **NACPME, British Council, Medlock Street, Manchester M15 4AA.**

Doctors who are overseas should contact the British Council in their own country; overseas-qualified doctors in the UK and those who do not have a British Council office in their own country should contact NACPME in Manchester.

It should be noted that the British Council does not place medical practitioners in hospital posts, nor will it offer a confidential report, reference or testimonial service. This service was entirely discontinued by the National Advice Centre in February 1989. Health authorities now wishing to employ overseas-qualified doctors should make their own arrangements to obtain confidential reports.

Overseas-qualified doctors are normally required to pass (or gain exemption from) a test of proficiency in English and of professional knowledge and competence before they can begin their first appointment in the United Kingdom. This test is conducted by the Professional and Linguistic Assessments Board (PLAB).

The examiners of the PLAB test are looking for proficiency in English and evidence that the applicant's medical knowledge is up to the standard of a Senior House Officer in a British hospital. We strongly advise all candidates to obtain up-to-date information on this exam from: The Overseas Registration Division, General Medical Council, 178–202 Great Portland Street, London W1N 6JE. Telephone 0171-580-7642. Not all non-UK qualified doctors are required to take this test so obtaining accurate information related to your specific qualifications and work experience is essential.

When your application to take the test has been accepted by the GMC they will then send you all relevant information including 'Advice to Candidates' which you should study very carefully. The standard required to pass the test is defined by the Board in the following terms: 'A candidate's command of the English language and professional knowledge and skill must be shown to be sufficient for him or her to undertake safely employment at first year Senior House Officer level in a British hospital'.

The PLAB test (which consists of 6 parts) has been devised so that examiners can assess a candidate's performance both in medicine and in the English language. A candidate must pass both the medical component and the English component of the test to satisfy the examiners and the GMC will notify a candidate by letter whether he has passed or failed. A pass means that on obtaining an educationally approved post in a training grade in a National Health Service hospital you may apply to the GMC for limited registration. If, however, you fail, you cannot become registered but you can apply to resit the exam at a future date. The total number of attempts permitted is limited.

Language Component:

    a) The Comprehension of Spoken English Examination (1 hour)
    b) The Written English Examination (1 hour)
    c) Part of the Oral Examination (total 20 mins)

Medical Component:

    d) The Multiple Choice Questions Examination (1½ hours)
    e) Clinical Problem Solving Examination (1 hour)
    f) The Photographic Material Examination (40 mins)
    g) The Oral Examination (viva)

The pass rate of this test is low (37% in 1993) and it is expensive to take. Overseas doctors should try to assess if they are up to the required medical and English language standard before applying to sit this difficult exam.

Medical knowledge and competence is tested by questions in:

    medicine (including medical specialties)
    surgery (including surgical specialties)
    obstetrics and gynaecology
    basic sciences (anatomy, physiology and pathology)

and your revision should aim to cover these subjects as thoroughly as possible. By providing full teaching explanations to the multiple choice questions, the authors of this book have tried to provide helpful revision material which can be used alongside standard textbooks for additional information.

This book has been written for doctors who need advice and help on the medical sections of the test. Those requiring help with the English sections should obtain the PasTest PLAB English books. No responsibility can be accepted by the publishers for inaccuracies and candidates should always apply for up-to-date information from the GMC.

The Multiple Choice Question Paper in the PLAB exam consists of 60 questions to be answered in 1½ hours, in other words you only have 1½ minutes in which to answer each question with its five answer options, A, B, C, D, E.

It is very important that you read the question (both stem and items) very carefully. Once you feel confident that you understand the question then you need to mark the computer card with your answer. Take great care not to mark the wrong boxes and think very carefully before filling in the answer card. Regard each item (A, B, C, D, E) as being independent of the other items – each refers to a specific piece of knowledge. The stem and each item make up a statement. You are required to indicate whether you regard this statement as 'True' or 'False' and you are also able to indicate 'Don't know'. Look only at the single statement when answering – disregard all the other statements presented in the question. They have nothing to do with the item you are concentrating on.

MCQ terminology

The wording of a multiple choice question may contain a 'trigger' word which is worthy of careful interpretation.

Always: Invariably and without a single exception. (The answer to this is usually false.)

Only: The answer is almost always false.

Never: Not in one single person nor on one single occasion (usually false).

Usually: In the majority of cases. (At least 50% and strictly speaking more than 50%.) Other words with a similar meaning are: mostly, generally, commonly, mainly, predominantly, principally.

Probably: Something that is likely.

Possible/May/Can: Occurs in some instances.

Frequent/Often: Occurs regularly, is a regular occurrence.

Rarely: Refers to something that is definitely unusual and uncommon. Other words with a similar meaning are: infrequently, occasionally.

A characteristic feature: A feature that occurs with sufficient frequency as to be of some diagnostic significance. Absence of the feature might make you doubt the diagnosis.

A typical feature: A feature that you would expect to be present (this is more or less the same as a characteristic feature).

A recognized feature: One that has been reported and that is a fact that a candidate would reasonably be expected to know. Thus, all 'characteristic' features are 'recognized', but many 'recognized' features could not be described as 'characteristic'.

Is associated with: A feature which is well recognized but not necessarily common. A feature which occurs more frequently than by chance.

A pathognomonic feature: Refers to a feature which is found in that disorder and no other.

Marking your answer card

Your answer card will be read by an automatic document reader, which transfers the information it reads to a computer. It must therefore be filled out in accordance with the instructions. A sample answer card is shown on p xii. Record your answers by marking a heavy black line in the appropriate block by using the pencil provided in the examination hall.

Each block correctly shaded in scores +1 but each block incorrectly shaded in scores −1. If you don't know the answer then both blocks must be filled in (this scores 0).

With 60 questions to answer in 1½ hours this means 1½ minutes per question for thinking time *and* marking the computer answer card. Do not waste precious time at the official exam in familiarizing yourself with the computer boxes and how to mark them, you must practise this beforehand. Read the instructions at the top of your paper with great care and make sure that you understand them. Some candidates like to mark their answer card as they go through the test and others like to mark their question papers and leave time at the end to transfer marks to the answer card. If you decide to mark your answers first of all on the question paper it is **vital** that you leave enough time to transfer your answers onto the computer card before the end of the allowed time of 1½ hours. You will not be given extra time at the exam in which to transfer your marks onto the computer card.

If you are not sure about a particular answer (for example, question 14) and wish to return to it at the end, be sure that you do not mark the answer to 15 in the empty boxes relating to question 14. You can put a tiny mark against the number on your answer card indicating that you wish to return and this will remind you to leave it blank so you can return to it at the end.

Careless marking of the printed answer card is probably one of the commonest causes of rejection by the document reader. You must fill in the blocks on the official answer card as strongly and neatly as you can.

To guess or not to guess

Candidates are frequently uncertain whether or not to guess the answer to a question they are not sure about. However, a clear distinction must be made between a wild guess and an educated guess which is based on a process of reasoning by which you attempt to work out an answer that is not immediately apparent by using first principles and drawing on your knowledge and experience. Wild guesses should *not* be made. You might be lucky, but if you are totally ignorant of the answer there is an equal chance that you will be wrong and thus lose marks. This is not a chance that is worth taking, and you should indicate 'Don't know' if you do not know the answer.

To repeat the important points of technique:

1. Read the question very carefully and be sure you understand it.
2. Use reasoning to work out answers, but if you really do not know the answer and cannot work it out then indicate 'Don't know' by filling in both blocks A and a.
3. If you are pretty sure that you know the right answer but not absolutely certain, then it is *definitely* worth guessing.
4. Do not spend too long on problem questions, move on and come back to them when you have completed the rest of the paper.
5. Mark your answers on the card clearly, correctly and accurately with the pencil provided.
6. Keep an eye on your watch and be sure to complete the paper and fill in your answer card before the end of the 1½ hours allowed.

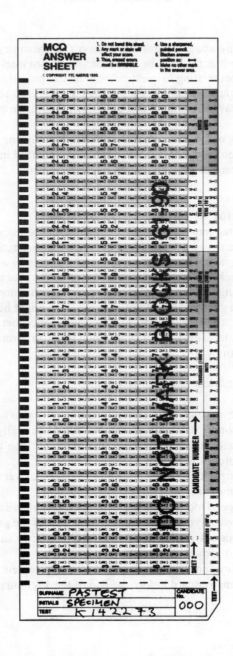

Sample computer card, reproduced by kind permission of the GMC.

THE MULTIPLE CHOICE QUESTION PAPER

INSTRUCTIONS

In order to help PLAB candidates revise for this difficult examination we have tried to follow as closely as possible the content and format of the official examination. Each question has an answer and teaching explanation which should provide a good basis for successful revision.

We suggest that you work on each set of 60 multiple choice questions as though it was a real PLAB test. In other words time yourself to spend no more than 1½ hours on each practice exam and do not obtain help from books, notes or persons while working on each test. Plan to take this practice exam at a time when you will be undisturbed for a minimum of 1½ hours. Choose a well lit location free from distractions, keep your desk clear of other books or papers, have a clock or watch clearly visible with a rubber and two well sharpened grade B pencils to hand.

As you work through each question in this book be sure and mark a tick or cross (True or False) in the answer boxes against each question. If you do not know the answer then leave the answer box blank. Thus when you have completed your paper you can mark your own answers with the help of the answers and explanations given at the end of the book. Do not be tempted to look at the questions before sitting down to take each test as this will not then represent a mock exam.

When you have finished an exam be sure to go back over your answers until the 1½ hours is over. When your time is up you can then mark your answers and study the teaching explanations carefully so as to learn from your mistakes. Give yourself +1 for every correct answer, –1 for every incorrect answer and 0 for an unanswered (don't know) question. Put a mark clearly on the book wherever you put a wrong answer and this will help you with your final revision as the official exam grows nearer.

Good luck with your revision.

PRACTICE EXAM 1

60 questions: Time allowed 1½ hours.
Mark your answers with a tick (True) or a cross (False) in the box provided.
Leave the box blank for 'Don't know'.

1   Dysmetria is a recognized finding in:

- ☐   A   Parkinson's disease
- ☐   B   Wilson's disease
- ☐   C   Huntington's chorea
- ☐   D   Friedreich's ataxia
- ☐   E   thrombosis of the posterior inferior cerebellar artery

2   The following drugs may cause the nephrotic syndrome:

- ☐   A   phenytoin
- ☐   B   prednisolone
- ☐   C   penicillamine
- ☐   D   colchicine
- ☐   E   gold

3   The following investigations are helpful in the diagnosis of sarcoidosis:

- ☐   A   scalene node biopsy
- ☐   B   bronchial lavage
- ☐   C   skeletal X-ray
- ☐   D   Kveim test
- ☐   E   Mantoux test

4   Thiazide diuretics

- ☐   A   relieve oedema
- ☐   B   are appropriate in cases of heart failure
- ☐   C   decrease aldosterone
- ☐   D   should be given in large doses
- ☐   E   may give rise to hyperkalaemia

5 Characteristic results of severe folate deficiency include:

- ☐ A steatorrhoea
- ☐ B a leukoerythroblastic anaemia
- ☐ C subacute combined degeneration of the spinal cord
- ☐ D hypersegmentation of the nuclei of the polymorphonuclear leucocytes
- ☐ E an increase in the total iron binding capacity of the blood

6 Raised serum cholesterol occurs in

- ☐ A diabetes mellitus
- ☐ B myxoedema
- ☐ C pancreatitis
- ☐ D oral contraceptive use
- ☐ E nephrotic syndrome

7 In travellers' diarrhoea

- ☐ A the attack is self-limiting
- ☐ B specific antimicrobial treatment is indicated
- ☐ C intravenous fluids are usually required
- ☐ D persisting mild diarrhoea suggests amoebiasis
- ☐ E diphenoxylate hydrochloride is often prescribed

8 Macrocytic anaemia is found in

- ☐ A post-gastrectomy syndromes
- ☐ B steatorrhoea
- ☐ C Crohn's disease
- ☐ D acute ulcerative colitis
- ☐ E carcinoma of the sigmoid colon

9 Hypokalaemia

- ☐ A aggravates digoxin toxicity
- ☐ B is common in alkalosis
- ☐ C causes a peaked 'p' wave
- ☐ D is a complication of thiazide therapy
- ☐ E is a feature of diabetes insipidus

10   Eosinophilia is characteristic of

- ☐ A   Hodgkin's disease
- ☐ B   hookworm infestation
- ☐ C   systemic lupus erythematosus
- ☐ D   toxoplasmosis
- ☐ E   motor neurone disease

11   Urinary tract infection

- ☐ A   is about six times more common in women than in men
- ☐ B   is rarely caused by staphylococci
- ☐ C   is often caused by anaerobic organisms
- ☐ D   is associated with a bacterial count of more than 100,000 organisms/ml of urine
- ☐ E   is often treated before the results of laboratory tests are received

12   Arthropathy is associated with

- ☐ A   psoriasis
- ☐ B   brucellosis
- ☐ C   sarcoidosis
- ☐ D   amyloidosis
- ☐ E   hyperlipidaemia

13   The Schilling test

- ☐ A   requires marrow to be aspirated from the sternum
- ☐ B   involves labelling with radioactive chromium
- ☐ C   can determine the rate at which red cells are destroyed
- ☐ D   may confirm a diagnosis of pernicious anaemia
- ☐ E   sometimes indicates the need for splenectomy

14   The following drugs are effective in prophylaxis of classical migraine:

- ☐ A   ergotamine
- ☐ B   clonidine
- ☐ C   propranolol
- ☐ D   pizotifen
- ☐ E   carbamazepine

15   The following conditions are associated with an increased incidence of cutaneous malignancy:

☐ A acanthosis nigricans
☐ B leucoplakia
☐ C solar keratosis
☐ D Bowen's disease
☐ E squamous papilloma

16   Enlargement of cardiac size is usually seen in chest radiography of patients with

☐ A uncomplicated mitral stenosis
☐ B pericardial effusion
☐ C aortic regurgitation
☐ D congestive cardiomyopathy
☐ E Addison's disease

17   Pulmonary atelectasis may be due to

☐ A alcohol abuse
☐ B chronic bronchitis
☐ C asthma
☐ D a tight bandage over an upper abdominal wound
☐ E vomiting

18   Anorexia nervosa is associated with

☐ A decreased plasma concentration of LH
☐ B fine hairs on the back
☐ C decreased physical activity
☐ D women who are postmenopausal
☐ E hypokalaemia

19 Recognized features of raised intracranial pressure include

- ☐ A third nerve palsy
- ☐ B dilatation of the pupil
- ☐ C VII nerve palsy
- ☐ D V nerve palsy
- ☐ E convulsions

20 Hypothyroidism

- ☐ A is most commonly caused by iatrogenic factors
- ☐ B may be caused by a pituitary deficiency of thyroid stimulating hormone
- ☐ C may result in hypoplasia of the brain
- ☐ D can be arrested and even reversed in some cases of cretinism
- ☐ E may be associated with a pot belly

21 Recognized features of aspirin poisoning include

- ☐ A respiratory acidosis
- ☐ B metabolic alkalosis
- ☐ C the need for gastrointestinal lavage
- ☐ D a good response to acetylcystine
- ☐ E gastric atony

22 Recognized symptoms and signs of the thalassaemias include

- ☐ A severe jaundice
- ☐ B mouth ulcers
- ☐ C hypertension
- ☐ D cardiac failure
- ☐ E cholelithiasis

23 **A woman has polycystic disease of the kidneys. It is more likely than would have been expected by chance that she will**

☐ A have children with the disease
☐ B die of a subarachnoid haemorrhage
☐ C have episodes of haematuria
☐ D suffer from urolithiasis
☐ E develop carcinoma of the kidney

24 **Recognized findings in bacterial meningitis include the following CSF results:**

☐ A increased cell count
☐ B increased glucose
☐ C increased protein
☐ D increased lymphocytes
☐ E increased bacteria

25 **Recognized causes of facial nerve palsy include**

☐ A chronic otitis media
☐ B stapedectomy
☐ C parotidectomy
☐ D parotid sialography
☐ E temporal lobe epilepsy

26 **Finger clubbing is a characteristic feature of**

☐ A rheumatoid arthritis
☐ B carcinoma of the bronchus
☐ C fibrosing alveolitis
☐ D chronic bronchitis
☐ E cystic fibrosis

27 In managing a case of cardiac arrest

- [ ] A asystole is treated with a defibrillator
- [ ] B DC shock is preferable to AC shock
- [ ] C maintenance of the airway is the first priority
- [ ] D 100% O_2 should never be given
- [ ] E adrenaline should be injected directly into the cardiac muscle

28 Recognized complications of lymphomas include

- [ ] A production of monoclonal immunoglobin light chains
- [ ] B autoimmune haemolytic anaemia
- [ ] C hypercalcaemia
- [ ] D cryptococcal meningitis
- [ ] E paraplegia

29 The following drugs are associated with peripheral neuropathy:

- [ ] A phenobarbitone
- [ ] B baclofen
- [ ] C pilocarpine
- [ ] D phenytoin
- [ ] E dobutamine

30 The following vaccines are cultured in eggs:

- [ ] A smallpox
- [ ] B rubella
- [ ] C yellow fever
- [ ] D polio (Sabin)
- [ ] E polio (Salk)

31 The normal infant

- ☐ A can fix his eyes on moving objects at 4 weeks
- ☐ B can smile at his mother in response to overtures at 6 weeks
- ☐ C can maintain his head horizontally when held in the prone position by 8 weeks
- ☐ D can vocalize if talked to at 8 weeks
- ☐ E turns his head to sounds at 8 weeks

32 Henoch-Schönlein purpura may be distinguished from post-streptococcal nephritis by the following findings:

- ☐ A swollen joints
- ☐ B high temperature
- ☐ C red cell casts in the urine
- ☐ D abdominal pain
- ☐ E melaena

33 Features supporting a diagnosis of acute appendicitis in a five-year-old boy with tenderness in the right iliac fossa include

- ☐ A pain felt in the right iliac fossa on pressing the left iliac fossa
- ☐ B preceding umbilical pain
- ☐ C more than ten white cells per high power field in the urine
- ☐ D bronchial breathing at the right lung base
- ☐ E severe diarrhoea

34 Regarding anaesthesia

- ☐ A oral anticoagulation is a contraindication to spinal anaesthesia
- ☐ B a minimum of 12 hours' starvation is necessary before gastric surgery
- ☐ C muscle relaxation is usually necessary for upper abdominal surgery
- ☐ D a triple lumen endotracheal tube may be necessary for intrathoracic surgery
- ☐ E a Swan Ganz catheter is directed into a branch of the pulmonary vein

35 Predisposing factors to a cerebral abscess include

☐ A acute endocarditis
☐ B bronchiectasis
☐ C cyanotic congenital heart disease
☐ D epilepsy
☐ E otitis media

36 The differential diagnoses of acute appendicitis include

☐ A food poisoning
☐ B perforated duodenal ulcer
☐ C 'mittelschmerz'
☐ D Crohn's disease
☐ E rectal prolapse

37 The use of prophylactic antibiotics for colonic surgery can produce

☐ A diarrhoea
☐ B pseudomembranous colitis
☐ C fungal infection of the colon
☐ D thrombocytopenia
☐ E iron deficiency anaemia

38 Non-suppurative otitis media

☐ A is especially common in children with cleft palate
☐ B is a cause of painful deafness in childhood
☐ C may present as learning or behavioural difficulties in childhood
☐ D may be complicated by facial palsy
☐ E is characterized by a sterile middle ear effusion

39 Late complications of gastric operations include

- ☐ A duodenal fistula ('blow out')
- ☐ B steatorrhoea
- ☐ C tuberculosis
- ☐ D calcium deficiency
- ☐ E lag storage glycosuria

40 In hypospadias

- ☐ A treatment should take place after the child is seven years old
- ☐ B circumcision is a recognized treatment
- ☐ C the meatus is most commonly situated on the penile shaft
- ☐ D chordee cause the penis to bend downwards (ventrally)
- ☐ E surgical correction is usually required

41 Characteristically Paget's disease of the nipple

- ☐ A presents bilaterally
- ☐ B is associated with an underlying ductal carcinoma of the breast
- ☐ C occurs during lactation
- ☐ D has a poor prognosis
- ☐ E does not have any specific histological features

42 Gallstones

- ☐ A are related to use of the oral contraceptive pill
- ☐ B may be silent throughout life
- ☐ C may cause small bowel obstruction
- ☐ D are more common in patients with iron deficiency anaemia
- ☐ E are usually present in carcinoma of the gallbladder

43 The following conditions predispose to skin cancer

- ☐ A lentigo maligna
- ☐ B Bowen's disease
- ☐ C lupus erythematosus
- ☐ D chronic leg ulcer
- ☐ E acanthosis nigricans

44 Paralytic ileus

- ☐ A causes diffuse distension throughout the small and large bowel
- ☐ B occurs early in strangulated inguinal hernia
- ☐ C causes air beneath the diaphragm
- ☐ D may occur following abdominal surgery
- ☐ E can be caused by fracture of the thoracolumbar spine

45 Actinomycosis

- ☐ A is caused by a Gram-negative rod
- ☐ B affects the ileocaecal region
- ☐ C is treated with metronidazole
- ☐ D may cause sinus formation
- ☐ E may affect the mandible

46 The following conditions predispose to oesophageal cancer

- ☐ A Plummer-Vinson syndrome
- ☐ B achalasia
- ☐ C female sex
- ☐ D reflux oesophagitis
- ☐ E coeliac disease

47 Flail chest

- ☐ A may result from fracture of a single rib
- ☐ B causes paradoxical chest wall movement
- ☐ C usually requires positive pressure ventilation
- ☐ D usually requires wiring of the rib fractures
- ☐ E rarely results in pneumothorax

48 Dupuytren's contracture

- ☐ A is associated with skin nodules
- ☐ B pulls the first and second fingers into the palm
- ☐ C may have an hereditary basis
- ☐ D lends itself readily to surgical correction
- ☐ E can necessitate amputation

49   An abortion is inevitable when

- ☐   A   the internal cervical os opens
- ☐   B   the products of conception are passed
- ☐   C   pregnancy tests are negative
- ☐   D   excessive bleeding occurs
- ☐   E   the external cervical os opens

50   Genito-urinary fistulae are a recognized feature of the following conditions:

- ☐   A   radiotherapy
- ☐   B   carcinoma of the cervix
- ☐   C   hysterectomy
- ☐   D   difficult childbirth
- ☐   E   herpes infection

51   An abdominal X-ray of a pregnant woman

- ☐   A   carries a risk to the foetus if taken in the third trimester
- ☐   B   is more reliable than ultrasound at determining congenital abnormalities
- ☐   C   usually shows ossification of upper tibial epiphysis at 39 weeks of pregnancy
- ☐   D   showing placental calcification confirms postmaturity
- ☐   E   provides reliable assessment of placenta position

52   Eclampsia

- ☐   A   rarely occurs in multiparous patients
- ☐   B   is more common antepartum than postpartum in the United Kingdom
- ☐   C   can cause reversible neurological deficit
- ☐   D   should be managed in a dark room
- ☐   E   causes hyperreflexia

53 Postpartum haemorrhage

- [ ] A is defined as blood loss in excess of 250 ml postpartum
- [ ] B is more commonly seen in those patients with antepartum haemorrhage
- [ ] C is associated with multiple pregnancy
- [ ] D can be predisposed by platelet deficiency
- [ ] E is reduced by active management of the third stage of labour

54 Uterine fibroids in pregnancy

- [ ] A are asymptomatic in most cases
- [ ] B may present with abdominal pain
- [ ] C may undergo red degeneration
- [ ] D lead to an increased risk of antepartum haemorrhage
- [ ] E should be removed surgically if they become symptomatic

55 Stress incontinence can be caused by

- [ ] A multiple sclerosis
- [ ] B alteration of the urethrovesical angle
- [ ] C a rectocele
- [ ] D myasthenia gravis
- [ ] E cystocele

56 Vulval ulceration may be due to

- [ ] A the herpes virus
- [ ] B squamous cell carcinoma
- [ ] C syphilis
- [ ] D atrophic vulvitis
- [ ] E lymphogranuloma inguinale

57 Human placental lactogen

☐ A is produced by the syncitiotrophoblast
☐ B is of value in predicting foetal size
☐ C concentration in maternal plasma increases as pregnancy progresses
☐ D is an insulin antagonist
☐ E is detectable only from the 12th week of pregnancy

58 Monilial infection of the vagina

☐ A is caused by a fungus
☐ B is caused by a protozoa
☐ C is a common cause of pruritus vulvae
☐ D can co-exist with *Trichomonas vaginalis*
☐ E can be treated with ampicillin

59 The following conditions must be met before applying forceps:

☐ A the head must be engaged
☐ B the bladder must be emptied
☐ C the cervix must be fully dilated
☐ D the foetus must be viable
☐ E contractions must have stopped

60 The diagnosis of secondary infertility indicates that

☐ A sterility is secondary to a medical condition
☐ B no living children have been produced
☐ C pregnancy has previously occurred
☐ D the infertility may be reversible
☐ E the infertility is due to secondary syphilis

END OF EXAM 1

Go over your answers until your time is up. Answers and teaching notes are on page 74.

PRACTICE EXAM 2

60 questions: Time allowed 1½ hours.
Mark your answers with a tick (True) or a cross (False) in the box provided.
Leave the box blank for 'Don't know'.

1 The following are recognized auscultatory findings in the conditions stated:

- [ ] A late systolic murmur – hypertrophic obstructive cardiomyopathy
- [ ] B fourth heart sound – atrial fibrillation
- [ ] C exaggerated splitting of the second heart sound – atrial septal defect
- [ ] D venous hum – persistent ductus arteriosus
- [ ] E pansystolic murmur – infarction of a mitral papillary muscle

2 The following conditions are of autosomal recessive inheritance:

- [ ] A myotonic dystrophy
- [ ] B myotonia congenita
- [ ] C Gilbert's syndrome
- [ ] D nephrogenic diabetes insipidus
- [ ] E tuberous sclerosis

3 A raised alkaline phosphatase is a recognized feature of the following conditions:

- [ ] A chronic active hepatitis
- [ ] B common bile duct obstruction
- [ ] C osteomalacia
- [ ] D myelomatosis
- [ ] E vitamin D resistant rickets

4 Recognized features of systemic lupus erythematosus include

- [ ] A eosinophilia
- [ ] B pericarditis
- [ ] C splenomegaly
- [ ] D arthritis
- [ ] E butterfly rash

5 Features of tuberculosis include

☐ A erythema marginatum
☐ B erythema nodosum
☐ C conjunctivitis
☐ D haematuria
☐ E arachnodactyly

6 Common incompatibility reactions in blood transfusions include

☐ A tachycardia
☐ B rigors
☐ C loin pain
☐ D transient jaundice
☐ E oliguria

7 Splenomegaly is seen in

☐ A miliary tuberculosis
☐ B sarcoidosis
☐ C interstitial fibrosis
☐ D pneumoconiosis
☐ E Caisson's disease

8 The bleeding time is characteristically prolonged in

☐ A haemophilia
☐ B Christmas disease
☐ C von Willebrand's disease
☐ D Factor XII deficiency
☐ E immune thrombocytopenic purpura

9 Cough is a recognized feature of the following

☐ A left ventricular failure
☐ B asthma
☐ C diazepam overdose
☐ D bronchitis
☐ E nervous tension

10 Conditions which are more commonly seen in males than in females include

☐ A ankylosing spondylitis
☐ B polyarteritis nodosa
☐ C mitral stenosis
☐ D coarctation of the aorta
☐ E congenital pyloric stenosis

11 The following conditions are premalignant:

☐ A melanosis coli
☐ B polyposis coli
☐ C ulcerative colitis
☐ D lichen sclerosus
☐ E Peyronie's disease of the penis

12 Recognized causes of vertigo include

☐ A anxiety
☐ B mumps
☐ C diplopia
☐ D syringobulbia
☐ E quinine

13 The following suggest an acute confusional state rather than dementia

☐ A disorientation of time and place
☐ B loss of short term memory
☐ C fluctuating conscious level
☐ D gradual onset
☐ E sixth nerve palsy

14 Recognized causes of purpura include

- [ ] A scurvy
- [ ] B haemophilia
- [ ] C idiopathic thrombocytopenic purpura
- [ ] D streptococcal sore throat
- [ ] E nephritis

15 A unilateral shrunken kidney may be found in

- [ ] A renal artery stenosis
- [ ] B chronic pyelonephritis
- [ ] C polyarteritis nodosa
- [ ] D tuberculosis
- [ ] E nephroblastoma

16 Recognized causes of extensor plantar response with loss of ankle jerk include

- [ ] A tabes dorsalis
- [ ] B taboparesis
- [ ] C generalized paralysis of the insane
- [ ] D subacute combined degeneration of the cord
- [ ] E syringomyelia

17 Pure B cell defects

- [ ] A are autosomal recessive
- [ ] B may be asymptomatic
- [ ] C are the most common type of primary specific immunodeficiency disorder
- [ ] D may be treated by human foetal thymus implantation
- [ ] E are usually fatal in infancy

18 Generalized wasting of the small muscles of the hand occurs in

- ☐ A carpal tunnel syndrome
- ☐ B motor neurone disease
- ☐ C rheumatoid arthritis
- ☐ D atherosclerosis
- ☐ E metastatic carcinoma

19 A 25-year-old woman presented with polyuria and polydipsia. The following features are relevant to the diagnosis:

- ☐ A lithium therapy
- ☐ B treatment with carbamazepine
- ☐ C bilateral hilar lymphadenopathy on the chest X-ray
- ☐ D hypertension, proximal muscle weakness and tetany
- ☐ E anaemia, hypertension and Kussmaul's respiration

20 In blood transfusion, complications are commonly a result of

- ☐ A giving too much blood
- ☐ B giving blood that is too cool
- ☐ C failure to use millipore filters in cases of large transfusion
- ☐ D failure to use a fresh vein at frequent intervals
- ☐ E administering packed cells more than six hours after their preparation

21 Horner's syndrome

- ☐ A can be caused by thrombosis of the posterior inferior cerebellar artery
- ☐ B can occur after operation for tetralogy of Fallot
- ☐ C is a non-metastatic extra pulmonary manifestation of oat cell carcinoma of the lung
- ☐ D is a recognized feature of syringomyelia
- ☐ E produces complete ptosis in some cases

19

22 The following are recognized features of scurvy:

- [ ] A gum hyperplasia
- [ ] B subperiosteal haemorrhage
- [ ] C blue line on the gums
- [ ] D loss of teeth
- [ ] E a raw tongue

23 Ichthyosis vulgaris

- [ ] A has a fish-type of scale
- [ ] B occurs in childhood
- [ ] C is most common on the scalp
- [ ] D has a diagnostic histology
- [ ] E may have corneal opacities as an associated clinical finding

24 The following features are helpful in the differential diagnosis of dysphagia:

- [ ] A Raynaud's phenomenon
- [ ] B tongue fibrillation
- [ ] C koilonychia
- [ ] D tylosis palmaris
- [ ] E treatment with immunosuppressive drugs

25 In septic shock there may be

- [ ] A no need for the results of blood cultures
- [ ] B a history of corticosteroid therapy
- [ ] C anxiety
- [ ] D cyanosis
- [ ] E warm peripheries

26 A peaked 'p' wave may be caused by

- [ ] A hypertrophy of the right atrium
- [ ] B hypertrophy of the left atrium
- [ ] C tricuspid valve stenosis
- [ ] D pulmonary hypertension
- [ ] E death of heart muscle

27   Periorbital oedema is a recognized sign in

☐ A   acute glomerulonephritis
☐ B   acute iritis
☐ C   dermatomyositis
☐ D   ophthalmic Graves' disease
☐ E   progressive systemic sclerosis

28   Recognized features of acromegaly include

☐ A   large tongue
☐ B   difficulty with dentures
☐ C   headache
☐ D   decreased visual fields
☐ E   spade shaped hands

29   Recognized features of tricyclic antidepressant therapy include

☐ A   ataxia
☐ B   jaundice
☐ C   arrhythmias
☐ D   coma
☐ E   convulsions

30   Noradrenaline causes

☐ A   pupil dilatation
☐ B   vasoconstriction
☐ C   contraction of sphincters
☐ D   increased blood pressure
☐ E   breakdown of liver glycogen

31   Growth retardation may be due to

☐ A   congenital heart disease
☐ B   hypoparathyroidism
☐ C   hypothyroidism
☐ D   malnutrition
☐ E   psychological causes

32 Recognized features of cerebral spastic quadraplegia in infants include

- ☐ A hyperbilirubinaemia
- ☐ B intracranial malignancy
- ☐ C high stepping gait
- ☐ D positive family history
- ☐ E multiple pregnancy

33 Retarded bone age may be due to

- ☐ A cretinism
- ☐ B scurvy
- ☐ C rickets
- ☐ D Down's syndrome
- ☐ E malignancy

34 Onychogryphosis

- ☐ A is a deformity of the nail bed
- ☐ B may require excision of the nail bed
- ☐ C mainly occurs as a complication of systemic disease
- ☐ D is often painless
- ☐ E frequently occurs in young people

35 Large bowel obstruction

- ☐ A is usually due to diverticular disease
- ☐ B is more likely to occur in the elderly
- ☐ C causes steatorrhoea
- ☐ D quickly gives rise to vomiting
- ☐ E may be caused by hypokalaemia

36 **The following will present as scrotal swellings that transilluminate, in which the testis may be felt separately from the swelling and where the spermatic cord may be felt above ('got above') the swelling:**

- ☐ A inguinal hernia
- ☐ B patent processus vaginalis
- ☐ C encysted hydrocoele of the cord
- ☐ D epididymal cyst
- ☐ E tuberculous epididymo-orchitis

37 **In upper gastrointestinal bleeding**

- ☐ A gastric erosions are a common cause
- ☐ B surgery is indicated if initial haemoglobin is less than 10 g/dl
- ☐ C surgery should be performed more readily in older patients
- ☐ D a visible vessel on endoscopy indicates an increased risk of rebleeding
- ☐ E haematemesis is more common than melaena from a bleeding duodenal ulcer

38 **Predisposing factors for carcinoma of the bladder include**

- ☐ A aniseed
- ☐ B bladder diverticulum
- ☐ C schistosomiasis
- ☐ D malaria
- ☐ E naphthalene exposure

39 **In brachial plexus injury**

- ☐ A a complete injury causes spastic paralysis
- ☐ B Klumpke (Déjérine) paralysis is associated with a claw hand
- ☐ C palsy of the cervical sympathetic nerves is a good sign
- ☐ D the prognosis in general is very good
- ☐ E some varieties are due to birth injury

40 Carcinoma of the larynx

- ☐ A drains to the cervical lymph nodes
- ☐ B is usually a squamous cell carcinoma
- ☐ C should be suspected in a patient with hoarseness lasting for longer than 14 days
- ☐ D presents early if the tumours are subglottic
- ☐ E is commoner in males than females

41 A ganglion on the dorsum of the foot

- ☐ A is translucent
- ☐ B arises from a nerve sheath
- ☐ C is said to resemble a melon seed
- ☐ D can be treated by injection
- ☐ E arises from the tendon sheath

42 Renal cell carcinoma is associated with

- ☐ A persistent pyrexia
- ☐ B tumour embolism
- ☐ C polycythaemia
- ☐ D hydrocoele
- ☐ E bone metastases

43 Amoebic liver abscesses

- ☐ A are multiple in most cases
- ☐ B can be detected early
- ☐ C are common in the right lobe of the liver
- ☐ D should be treated surgically
- ☐ E do not occur without intestinal amoebiasis

44   In testicular tumours

- [ ] A   the diagnosis may be established by percutaneous biopsy
- [ ] B   the cells in seminoma resemble spermatocytes
- [ ] C   teratoma of the testis arises from the rete testis
- [ ] D   gynaecomastia and a positive pregnancy test are features
- [ ] E   inguinal lymph nodes may be affected early in the disease

45   The following statements are true about pancreatitis

- [ ] A   men are affected more often than women
- [ ] B   renal failure is a common cause of death
- [ ] C   pseudocyst formation does not usually occur within two months
- [ ] D   hypocalcaemia may occur
- [ ] E   surgery is usually indicated

46   Osteomyelitis

- [ ] A   occurs in the epiphysis
- [ ] B   is usually caused by *Staphylococcus aureus*
- [ ] C   requires early surgical treatment
- [ ] D   gives rise to bone necrosis
- [ ] E   causes radiological changes early

47   Congenital displacement of the hip

- [ ] A   can be detected at birth
- [ ] B   is more common in boys than girls
- [ ] C   is more common following breech delivery
- [ ] D   is suggested by the appearance of the skin creases of the neonate
- [ ] E   results in a positive Trendelenburg sign by five months

48   In Colles' fracture, the distal fragment

- [ ] A   is disimpacted
- [ ] B   is medially angulated
- [ ] C   is dorsally angulated
- [ ] D   is supinated
- [ ] E   is displaced ventrally

49 Recognized causes of vulval irritation include

- ☐ A carcinoma of the body of the uterus
- ☐ B acute bartholinitis
- ☐ C trichomonal vaginitis
- ☐ D cervical erosion
- ☐ E excessive clothing

50 Recognized features of Sheehan's syndrome include

- ☐ A lethargy
- ☐ B weight loss
- ☐ C amenorrhoea
- ☐ D hypoproteinaemia
- ☐ E a coarse skin

51 Carcinoma of the cervix is associated with

- ☐ A nulliparous women
- ☐ B promiscuity
- ☐ C multiparity
- ☐ D orthodox Jewesses
- ☐ E oral contraceptives

52 Endometriosis

- ☐ A cannot be treated without surgery at some stage
- ☐ B may require diathermy cauterisation
- ☐ C can be treated with a course of progestogens in large dose for nine months
- ☐ D regresses rapidly when danazol is prescribed
- ☐ E is best treated with hysterectomy

53 Ethinyloestradiol may cause

- [ ] A nausea and vomiting
- [ ] B jaundice
- [ ] C elation
- [ ] D endometrial carcinoma in premenopausal women
- [ ] E sodium retention

54 Diaphragms

- [ ] A are associated with Dutch cap disease
- [ ] B may have coiled springs built into them
- [ ] C come in sizes from 50 mm to 90 mm
- [ ] D must always be inserted by a medically qualified person
- [ ] E should be resized at least once every three years

55 External cephalic version

- [ ] A means converting a breech presentation to a cephalic presentation
- [ ] B is contraindicated when the uterus contains a scar
- [ ] C may be complicated by premature delivery
- [ ] D may cause foetal bradycardia
- [ ] E cannot be performed after the 32nd week

56 During difficult breech delivery

- [ ] A delivery may be facilitated by fracturing the newborn's clavicle
- [ ] B the humerus is sometimes fractured
- [ ] C fractures of the femur are usually greenstick
- [ ] D perfect remodelling is usual, even if there is an initially moderate degree of angulation, following long bone fractures
- [ ] E soft tissue injuries to the neonate may later require exchange transfusion

57 Hydatidiform mole may be complicated by

☐ A salpingitis
☐ B coagulation defects
☐ C ectopic pregnancy
☐ D sepsis
☐ E choriocarcinoma

58 Generally accepted contraindications to therapy with combined oral contraceptive preparations include

☐ A varicose veins
☐ B generalized pruritus in a previous pregnancy
☐ C carcinoma of the breast
☐ D menorrhagia
☐ E previous history of thromboembolism

59 Causes of proteinuria in pregnancy include

☐ A chronic glomerulonephritis
☐ B uncomplicated essential hypertension
☐ C acute pyelonephritis
☐ D abruptio placentae without pre-eclampsia
☐ E diabetic nephropathy

60 In a pregnancy with an anencephalic foetus

☐ A polyhydramnios is often present
☐ B gestation may be prolonged
☐ C foetal adrenal hypoplasia is present
☐ D dystocia is common
☐ E the foetus is usually female

END OF EXAM 2

Go over your answers until your time is up. Answers and teaching notes are on page 87.

60 Questions: time allowed 1½ hours.
Mark your answers with a tick (True) or a cross (False) in the box provided.
Leave the box blank for 'Don't know'.

1   The following conditions are more common in males than females:

☐   A   patent ductus arteriosus
☐   B   polyarteritis nodosa
☐   C   polymyalgia rheumatica
☐   D   ankylosing spondylitis
☐   E   atrial septal defect

2   Hypercalcaemia is a feature of

☐   A   sarcoidosis
☐   B   osteoporosis
☐   C   Paget's disease
☐   D   secondary hyperparathyroidism
☐   E   adrenal failure

3   Recognized side effects of therapeutic doses of lithium salts include

☐   A   extrapyramidal manifestations
☐   B   renal failure
☐   C   hyperkinesia
☐   D   gum hypertrophy
☐   E   nystagmus

4   Diseases transmissible by blood transfusion include

☐   A   malaria
☐   B   rheumatoid arthritis
☐   C   viral hepatitis
☐   D   syphilis
☐   E   infectious mononucleosis

5   Primary haemochromatosis

☐   A   is a cause of macronodular cirrhosis
☐   B   causes skin pigmentation due to excess ferritin in the skin
☐   C   predisposes to the development of hepatic adenomas
☐   D   responds well to penicillamine therapy
☐   E   is associated with pyrophosphate arthropathy

6   In the treatment of Hodgkin's disease

☐   A   chemotherapy is the treatment of choice for localised disease
☐   B   radiotherapy is used only in cases of extensive disease
☐   C   accurate staging is very important
☐   D   remissions may be seen in up to 40% of cases
☐   E   bone marrow biopsy may be indicated

7   A wide pulse pressure is a recognized feature of

☐   A   complete heart block
☐   B   thyrotoxicosis
☐   C   persistent ductus arteriosus
☐   D   constrictive pericarditis
☐   E   mitral stenosis

8   The following are appropriate in the treatment of acute congestive glaucoma

☐   A   mydriatics
☐   B   miotics
☐   C   steroids
☐   D   acetazolamide
☐   E   pilocarpine

9   The following are recognized side effects of aspirin:

☐   A   tinnitus
☐   B   deafness
☐   C   mental confusion
☐   D   bronchospasm
☐   E   thrombocytopenia

10   Vitamin B12 deficiency is a recognized complication of

☐   A   co-trimoxazole therapy
☐   B   extensive psoriasis
☐   C   phenytoin therapy
☐   D   progressive systemic sclerosis affecting the bowel
☐   E   diverticular disease of the colon

11   The following manifestations of convulsive seizures are associated with the temporal lobe:

☐   A   localized muscle twitching
☐   B   localized numbness
☐   C   chewing movements
☐   D   visual hallucinations
☐   E   olfactory hallucinations

12   Recognized causes of male infertility include

☐   A   Klinefelter's syndrome
☐   B   dystrophia myotonica
☐   C   isolated growth hormone deficiency
☐   D   cystic fibrosis
☐   E   haemochromatosis

13 Tuberculosis

- ☐ A is most frequently due to *M. bovis*
- ☐ B may be due to isoniazid (INH) resistant organism
- ☐ C is almost always initiated by inhalation
- ☐ D may involve any organ
- ☐ E frequently involves the kidneys

14 Recognized causes of malabsorption include

- ☐ A ulcerative colitis
- ☐ B coeliac disease
- ☐ C diverticulosis
- ☐ D giardiasis
- ☐ E Meckel's diverticulum

15 Excitation may be caused by the following drugs:

- ☐ A amphetamines
- ☐ B phenobarbitone
- ☐ C tricyclic antidepressants
- ☐ D monoamine oxidase inhibitors
- ☐ E antihistamines

16 Neuropathic joints may be associated with the following conditions:

- ☐ A achondroplasia
- ☐ B syringomyelia
- ☐ C meningovascular syphilis
- ☐ D diabetes mellitus
- ☐ E septic arthritis

17 Schizophrenia is characteristically associated with

☐ A multiple personality
☐ B visual hallucinations
☐ C incoherent thinking
☐ D failure to appreciate the need for treatment
☐ E a sense that one is being manipulated

18 The following are features of constrictive pericarditis:

☐ A raised jugular venous pressure that falls during inspiration
☐ B splenomegaly
☐ C pericardial friction rub
☐ D calcification on the chest radiograph
☐ E atrial enlargement

19 The following are autosomal recessive:

☐ A Huntington's chorea
☐ B phenylketonuria
☐ C neurofibromatosis
☐ D haemophilia
☐ E haemochromatosis

20 Recognized causes of a third heart sound include

☐ A a normal physiological finding in children
☐ B heart failure
☐ C pericarditis
☐ D aortic stenosis
☐ E mitral incompetence

21 A patient with a lower motor neurone lesion of the facial nerve

☐ A cannot close the eye on the affected side
☐ B can wrinkle the forehead on both sides
☐ C protrudes the tongue with deviation to the affected side
☐ D may complain of hyperacusis
☐ E has absent corneal sensation in the eye on the affected side

22 Recognized causes of atrial fibrillation include

☐ A aortic stenosis
☐ B diabetes mellitus
☐ C thyrotoxicosis
☐ D rheumatic fever
☐ E Dressler's syndrome

23 Hyponatraemia

☐ A is a feature of the syndrome of inappropriate anti-diuretic hormone secretion
☐ B can result from longstanding diuretic therapy
☐ C produces a rise in blood pressure
☐ D is a feature of Conn's syndrome (primary hyperaldosteronism)
☐ E causes tetany

24 Characteristic features of papilloedema include

☐ A disc pallor
☐ B exaggeration of the physiological cup
☐ C retinal vessel engorgement
☐ D surrounding haemorrhage
☐ E visual loss beginning on the nasal side and moving to the temporal side

25 Iron deficiency anaemia

☐ A is often due to blood loss
☐ B may be caused by a chronic infection
☐ C is associated with a normal plasma iron level
☐ D is more common in adolescents than children
☐ E is about three times more common in women than men

26 Gout is

☐ A more common in men than women
☐ B a cause of renal calculi
☐ C a cause of acute arthritis
☐ D due to increased uric acid production
☐ E due to a deficiency of glucose 6 phosphatase

27 Alkaline phosphatase is raised in

☐ A myocardial infarction
☐ B osteomalacia
☐ C multiple myeloma
☐ D Paget's disease
☐ E acute cholecystitis

28 A 32-year-old woman is admitted to hospital with a three day history of fever, generalized lymphadenopathy and a macular rash over the trunk and legs. The following diagnoses are consistent with the clinical picture:

☐ A infectious mononucleosis
☐ B sarcoidosis
☐ C mumps
☐ D secondary syphilis
☐ E chickenpox

29 Concerning the anatomy of the heart these statements are true

- ☐ A the superior vena cava returns deoxygenated blood from the head and abdomen
- ☐ B the pulmonary valve regulates blood returning from the pulmonary veins
- ☐ C there are four pulmonary veins
- ☐ D the mitral valve regulates blood entering the left ventricle
- ☐ E the aortic valve regulates blood leaving the left ventricle

30 *Bacteroides* are

- ☐ A Gram positive
- ☐ B sporing
- ☐ C predominant in the lower intestine
- ☐ D always anaerobic
- ☐ E sensitive to lincomycin

31 Regarding neonatal intestinal obstruction

- ☐ A occasional bile stained vomiting can be disregarded
- ☐ B early abdominal distension is a prominent feature
- ☐ C passage of meconium excludes the condition
- ☐ D X-rays are not of much value
- ☐ E Hirschsprung's disease is more common in males than females

32 Regarding neurodevelopmental assessment of a normal child

- ☐ A at 20 weeks he can transfer from hand to hand
- ☐ B hearing assessment should be done in all children at 4 months of age
- ☐ C voluntary smile can be expected from 4 weeks of age
- ☐ D a 1-year-old child is expected to say two to three words with meaning
- ☐ E the anterior fontanelle should be closed by 15 months

33 In a child with primary nocturnal enuresis

- ☐ A fluid restriction is an effective treatment
- ☐ B the diagnosis should not be made before the child is 5 years old
- ☐ C there is a significant association with urinary tract infection
- ☐ D complete neurological examination is essential
- ☐ E desmopressin is an accepted form of treatment

34 Avascular necrosis is a recognized complication of a fracture of

- ☐ A the shaft of the femur
- ☐ B the subtrochanteric neck of the femur
- ☐ C the scaphoid
- ☐ D the shaft of the humerus
- ☐ E the tibia

35 Hammer toes

- ☐ A sometimes result from hallux valgus
- ☐ B affect the great toe in most cases
- ☐ C have hyperextended metatarsophalangeal and distal interphalangeal joints
- ☐ D are associated with callosities
- ☐ E are characterized by toe pads which do not contact the ground on standing

36 A closed fracture of the mid-shaft of the femur

- ☐ A leads to a fall in circulating blood volume
- ☐ B is a common cause of sciatic nerve injury
- ☐ C is a cause of haemarthrosis of the knee
- ☐ D may be followed by fat embolism
- ☐ E may follow joint replacement

37 A lignocaine–adrenaline mixture

- ☐ A may stop local arteriolar bleeding
- ☐ B is contraindicated in patients with cardiac problems
- ☐ C should not be given in combination with monoamine oxidase inhibitors
- ☐ D means smaller volumes of local anaesthetic solution can be administered
- ☐ E may cause end artery spasm and gangrene

38 Rest pain

- ☐ A frequently precedes gangrene
- ☐ B is often worse in the morning
- ☐ C most commonly affects the calf
- ☐ D may be intractable
- ☐ E is relieved by elevation

39 The incidence of deep vein thrombosis may be reduced by the following

- ☐ A use of a tourniquet
- ☐ B early mobilization
- ☐ C intermittent calf compression during surgery
- ☐ D the use of graduated compression stockings
- ☐ E perioperative hormones

40 A lump in the breast of a 35-year-old woman

- ☐ A should be investigated by mammography and fine needle aspiration cytology
- ☐ B is a cancer if axillary lymph nodes are enlarged
- ☐ C is a fibroadenoma if painful
- ☐ D may be recognized as a cyst on clinical examination
- ☐ E may fluctuate in size with the menstrual cycle

41 Dupuytren's contracture

☐ A is usually due to a contraction of the plantar aponeurosis
☐ B may be associated with Peyronie's disease
☐ C seldom affects the ring finger
☐ D is commoner in males than females
☐ E can be treated by physiotherapy

42 Postoperative complications of a prostatectomy include

☐ A incontinence
☐ B carcinoma of the prostate
☐ C ureteric stricture
☐ D retrograde ejaculation
☐ E epididymitis

43 Carcinoma of the tongue

☐ A is more common in smokers
☐ B is most frequently situated on the anterior two-thirds of the tongue
☐ C carries a better prognosis than carcinoma of the lip
☐ D may be treated by radiotherapy to preserve function
☐ E is commoner in men than women

44 Recognized complications of diverticular disease include

☐ A haemorrhage
☐ B pseudopolyp formation
☐ C colocutaneous fistula
☐ D pneumaturia
☐ E malignant change

45 An injury to the median nerve at the wrist results in

- ☐ A loss of sensation over the anatomical snuff box
- ☐ B paralysis of abductor pollicis brevis
- ☐ C paralysis of opponens pollicis
- ☐ D paralysis of all the dorsal interossei
- ☐ E loss of sensation over the palmar aspect of the middle finger

46 Recognized causes of fistula in ano include

- ☐ A leukaemia
- ☐ B diverticular disease
- ☐ C anorectal tumours
- ☐ D Crohn's disease
- ☐ E ischaemic colitis

47 A solitary palpable nodule of the thyroid

- ☐ A may be caused by a multinodular goitre
- ☐ B is likely to be malignant
- ☐ C is usually treated by thyroid lobectomy
- ☐ D is more common in men than women
- ☐ E may cause dysphagia

48 Cholelithiasis is more common in

- ☐ A Crohn's disease
- ☐ B pernicious anaemia
- ☐ C hereditary spherocytosis
- ☐ D patients with kidney stones
- ☐ E cirrhosis

49   Human colostrum

- ☐   A   is low in calories
- ☐   B   is low in protein
- ☐   C   is produced before birth
- ☐   D   is produced after birth
- ☐   E   contains antigens

50   A 30-year-old woman at 37 weeks' gestation has vaginal bleeding. Factors supporting a diagnosis of placental abruption include

- ☐   A   albuminuria
- ☐   B   absence of pain
- ☐   C   tenderness over the body of the uterus
- ☐   D   foetal malpresentation
- ☐   E   features of shock out of proportion to the amount of blood loss

51   Carcinoma of the body of the uterus

- ☐   A   occurs before the menopause in about 25% of cases
- ☐   B   may present early with a watery discharge
- ☐   C   is usually associated with pain
- ☐   D   commonly causes demonstrable enlargement of the uterus
- ☐   E   causes nodules to form on the labia minor and major

52   Secondary dysmenorrhoea

- ☐   A   is a term for painful intercourse
- ☐   B   may precede the menstrual flow
- ☐   C   is relieved by antispasmodics
- ☐   D   is characteristically associated with organic disease
- ☐   E   is often improved by dilatation of the cervix

53 Causes of vomiting in late pregnancy include

☐ A hiatus hernia
☐ B pre-eclamptic toxaemia
☐ C hyperemesis gravidarum
☐ D hydatidiform mole
☐ E acute pyelonephritis

54 Ectopic pregnancy

☐ A occurs in the Fallopian tubes in 95% of cases
☐ B may occur in the ovaries themselves
☐ C may be due to endometriosis
☐ D may be due to hormonal contraception
☐ E commonly results in tubal abortion 3 to 4 weeks after implantation

55 A 24-year-old woman in her second pregnancy presents in labour at 37 weeks with a prolapsed cord and the head presenting. The management alternatives include

☐ A monitor the foetal heart rate and then perform a forceps delivery at full dilatation
☐ B displace the foetal head from the cervix wall until an urgent Caesarean is performed
☐ C start an oxytocin intravenous infusion to expedite delivery
☐ D allow labour to continue if the cord is not pulsating and the foetal heart is not heard
☐ E perform a forceps delivery if the cervix is fully dilated

56 Polyhydramnios

☐ A is associated with an increased incidence in foetal malformations
☐ B may be caused by ascites
☐ C may be caused by an ovarian cyst
☐ D often leads to premature delivery
☐ E rarely presents in an acute form

57 The diagnosis of endometriosis

☐ A may be confused by the presence of pelvic inflammatory infection
☐ B may be suggested by chronic intestinal obstruction in a woman between 30 and 40 years of age
☐ C is supported by finding palpable non-tender pelvic nodules
☐ D is supported by multiple pregnancy
☐ E is frequently confirmed by the presence of poor bladder control

58 Recognized features of a premature infant include

☐ A weight less than 2500 g
☐ B susceptibility to birth trauma
☐ C hypoglycaemia
☐ D hypothermia
☐ E a dry wrinkled skin

59 Symptoms and signs of rhesus incompatibility include

☐ A profound anaemia *in utero*
☐ B oedema *in utero*
☐ C pleural effusion
☐ D ascites
☐ E hypertension

60 Characteristic features of rupture of the uterus in labour include

☐ A signs of intraperitoneal haemorrhage
☐ B vaginal haemorrhage
☐ C violent uterine contractions
☐ D a fall in systolic blood pressure
☐ E amniotic fluid embolism

END OF EXAM 3

Go over your answers until your time is up. Answers and teaching notes are on page 101.

60 Questions: time allowed 1½ hours.
Mark your answers with a tick (True) or a cross (False) in the box provided.
Leave the box blank for 'Don't know'.

1   The following cause pleural effusion:

☐   A   sarcoidosis
☐   B   pulmonary embolism
☐   C   pneumonia
☐   D   tuberculosis
☐   E   Dressler's syndrome

2   A facial butterfly rash is a characteristic feature of

☐   A   pityriasis rosea
☐   B   vitiligo
☐   C   scleroderma
☐   D   rosacea
☐   E   systemic lupus erythematosus

3   Increased levels of serum alkaline phosphatase are found in

☐   A   gout
☐   B   Paget's disease
☐   C   osteomalacia following gastrectomy
☐   D   senile osteoporosis
☐   E   acute pancreatitis

4   The following are consistent with the diagnosis of von Willebrand's disease

☐   A   prolonged bleeding time
☐   B   prolonged prothrombin time
☐   C   prolonged activated kaolin partial thromboplastin time (KPPT)
☐   D   low factor IX activity
☐   E   positive family history

5 Biguanides

- ☐ A are used in the treatment of diabetes mellitus
- ☐ B stimulate the pancreatic islet cells
- ☐ C are especially useful with obese patients
- ☐ D can cause lactic acidosis
- ☐ E are now rarely prescribed

6 Characteristic clinical features of meningitis are

- ☐ A headache relieved by movement
- ☐ B dimness of vision
- ☐ C positive Kernig's sign
- ☐ D hypothermia
- ☐ E relaxation of the spinal muscles

7 Factors which increase digoxin sensitivity include

- ☐ A old age
- ☐ B hypokalaemia
- ☐ C hyperthyroidism
- ☐ D poor health
- ☐ E pernicious anaemia

8 Recognized causes of hypertension include

- ☐ A Cushing's syndrome
- ☐ B Conn's syndrome
- ☐ C phaeochromocytoma
- ☐ D atherosclerosis
- ☐ E alcoholism

9   Hodgkin's disease with bone involvement may produce

☐ A pain
☐ B opacities
☐ C spinal cord compression
☐ D painful joints
☐ E fracture

10   Recognized causes of urinary incontinence in a 75-year-old woman include

☐ A acute urinary infection
☐ B acute cerebrovascular accident
☐ C faecal impaction
☐ D administration of chlorpromazine at night
☐ E vaginitis

11   Monocular loss of vision may be caused by

☐ A occipital lobe tumour
☐ B disseminated sclerosis (multiple sclerosis)
☐ C subdural haematoma
☐ D carotid artery atheroma
☐ E lead poisoning

12   Epileptic convulsions are a recognized complication of

☐ A inappropriate antidiuretic hormone secretion
☐ B withdrawal of long-term barbiturate treatment
☐ C depression
☐ D subdural haematoma
☐ E Down's syndrome

13 A narrow pulse pressure is a feature of

- ☐ A aortic stenosis
- ☐ B pulmonary stenosis
- ☐ C mitral stenosis
- ☐ D cor pulmonale
- ☐ E beri beri

14 Characteristic features of depression include

- ☐ A difficulty in waking up
- ☐ B worsening of the symptoms in the evening
- ☐ C constipation
- ☐ D loss of the ability to concentrate
- ☐ E bizarre hallucinations

15 Recognized causes of adrenal insufficiency include

- ☐ A corticosteroid therapy
- ☐ B idiopathic ACTH deficiency
- ☐ C Sheehan's syndrome
- ☐ D craniopharyngioma
- ☐ E trauma to adrenal tissue

16 Herniation of an intervertebral disc involving the first sacral nerve root causes

- ☐ A wasting of glutei on the affected side
- ☐ B sensory loss over the medial aspect of the leg
- ☐ C depression of the hamstring jerk
- ☐ D weakness of eversion of the foot
- ☐ E back pain induced by hyperextension of the hip with the knee flexed

17 Radioactive iodine therapy for thyrotoxicosis

- ☐ A slightly increases the risk of thyroid cancer
- ☐ B may cause peptic ulceration
- ☐ C may cause hypothyroidism
- ☐ D is contraindicated in pregnancy
- ☐ E may cause hypoparathyroidism

18 Recognized causes of generalized lymphadenopathy include

- ☐ A tuberculosis
- ☐ B Still's disease
- ☐ C brucellosis
- ☐ D syphilis
- ☐ E cat scratch disease

19 Cheyne-Stokes breathing

- ☐ A may be due to severe cardiac failure
- ☐ B is common in cases of bronchial obstruction
- ☐ C consists of very deep respirations
- ☐ D can result from terminal renal failure
- ☐ E could be a sign of cerebro-vascular accident

20 Prominent somatic signs of anxiety include

- ☐ A bradycardia
- ☐ B drooling
- ☐ C constipation
- ☐ D cold extremities
- ☐ E aching back

21 Chickenpox

☐ A is caused by a herpes virus
☐ B is characterized by an incubation period between 14 and 21 days
☐ C is an indication for acyclovir therapy in immunocompromised patients
☐ D produces skin lesions which undergo scarring
☐ E may be prevented by passive immunisation

22 Recognized presentations of carcinoma of the bronchus include

☐ A gynaecomastia
☐ B splenomegaly
☐ C hypokalaemia
☐ D myasthenia
☐ E painful ankles

23 In the following, the trachea may be shifted to the right:

☐ A left-sided pneumothorax
☐ B right-sided collapse of the lung
☐ C pericardial effusion
☐ D Hashimoto's thyroiditis
☐ E Hodgkin's disease

24 Recognized features of primary hyperparathyroidism include

☐ A peripheral neuropathy
☐ B depression
☐ C peptic ulcer
☐ D deafness
☐ E renal failure

25 The following statements are true of Hodgkin's lymphoma:

☐ A lymphocytic predominance is better than lymphocytic depletion
☐ B stage I is best treated by chemotherapy
☐ C splenectomy improves the prognosis
☐ D bone marrow biopsy may be useful for both the diagnosis and staging
☐ E the prognosis is very poor

26 Recognized features of myocardial infarction include

☐ A chest pain
☐ B pain radiating down the left arm
☐ C pericarditis
☐ D fever
☐ E blood stained sputum

27 Exposure to sunlight may induce or exacerbate

☐ A senile elastosis
☐ B seborrhoeic warts
☐ C chloasma
☐ D dermatitis herpetiformis
☐ E guttate psoriasis

28 In mitral valve disease the following indicate mitral stenosis rather than mitral incompetence:

☐ A soft first heart sound
☐ B third heart sound
☐ C atrial fibrillation
☐ D heaving apex beat
☐ E opening snap

29 Cholestatic jaundice may complicate therapy with

- ☐ A cortisone
- ☐ B chlorpromazine
- ☐ C penicillin
- ☐ D methyltestosterone
- ☐ E phenacetin

30 Azathioprine is

- ☐ A no longer used to prevent transplant rejection
- ☐ B less commonly prescribed than cyclophosphamide
- ☐ C given in larger doses when used in conjunction with allopurinol
- ☐ D helpful in the treatment of autoimmune diseases
- ☐ E frequently prescribed after the failure of corticosteroid therapy

31 Mental handicap is an important feature in

- ☐ A maple syrup disease
- ☐ B glycogen storage disorder type 1
- ☐ C galactosaemia
- ☐ D Duchenne muscular dystrophy
- ☐ E Marfan's syndrome

32 Turner's syndrome is associated with

- ☐ A normal breast development
- ☐ B an absent uterus
- ☐ C primary amenorrhoea
- ☐ D osteoporosis
- ☐ E hirsutism

33 Vulvovaginitis in a child

- [ ] A is usually caused by *Candida albicans*
- [ ] B occurs because of the lack of alkaline secretions on the vagina
- [ ] C may be gonococcal
- [ ] D is frequently caused by a foreign body in the vagina
- [ ] E may be caused by threadworms

34 Fournier's gangrene

- [ ] A characteristically appears suddenly in the midst of good health
- [ ] B is caused by testicular gangrene
- [ ] C is caused by staphylococci in most cases
- [ ] D can cause sloughing of the entire scrotum
- [ ] E is not usually associated with pyrexia

35 Mastectomy

- [ ] A is indicated for the treatment of multifocal ductal carcinoma *in situ*
- [ ] B may cause paralysis of serratus anterior muscle
- [ ] C is indicated for Paget's disease of the nipple without a palpable lump
- [ ] D can be followed by a latissimus dorsi reconstruction
- [ ] E requires routine ligation of the internal mammary artery

36 An intracerebral abscess

- [ ] A is a recognized complication of thyroid surgery
- [ ] B is a contraindication to lumbar puncture
- [ ] C is a complication of attic perforation
- [ ] D can cause a rapid rise in intracerebral pressure
- [ ] E classically causes neck stiffness and photophobia

37 Sigmoid volvulus

☐ A presents with a history of several days' absolute constipation
☐ B is often associated with a history of previous left sided abdominal pain
☐ C is a contraindication to sigmoidoscopy
☐ D usually affects the elderly or the institutionalised
☐ E is typically associated with vomiting

38 The following statements are true:

☐ A gastric cancer is more common in patients with blood group A
☐ B there is a relationship between gastric atrophy and gastric cancer
☐ C keratoacanthoma is a premalignant condition
☐ D gastric cancer most commonly affects the fundus
☐ E iron deficiency is the most likely cause of anaemia after gastric surgery

39 Tetanus

☐ A is caused by a Gram-negative organism
☐ B causes painless spasms
☐ C is treated by intravenous calcium gluconate
☐ D toxoid produces active immunity
☐ E in which a short gap occurs between the first symptom and the first reflex spasm has a good prognosis

40 Wound dehiscence after abdominal surgery

☐ A is rare, occurring in less than 5% of abdominal operations
☐ B usually occurs within five days of the operation
☐ C is commonly preceded by a serosanguinous discharge
☐ D may occur in uninfected wounds
☐ E is commoner after transverse incisions

41   Leucoplakia

- ☐   A   presents as keratinisation of the oral mucosa
- ☐   B   has a high malignant potential
- ☐   C   usually remits spontaneously
- ☐   D   may be due to poor dental hygiene
- ☐   E   has a greater risk of malignancy if it occurs on the floor of the mouth

42   In the treatment of burns

- ☐   A   escharotomy is indicated for circumferential burns
- ☐   B   prompt tracheostomy should be performed in inhalation injury
- ☐   C   compression can reduce scarring
- ☐   D   the greatest fluid loss occurs between 12 and 24 hours
- ☐   E   *Pseudomonas aeruginosa* is a common cause of sepsis

43   Which of the following may be true of breast cancer:

- ☐   A   most patients are cured if treated properly
- ☐   B   lymphoedema is a complication of treatment
- ☐   C   tamoxifen is useful only in postmenopausal women
- ☐   D   men with breast cancer have a better prognosis than women
- ☐   E   oophorectomy may be therapeutic

44   Abdominal aortic aneurysm

- ☐   A   may be associated with a popliteal aneurysm
- ☐   B   may present as renal colic
- ☐   C   is a familial condition
- ☐   D   should be treated by excision of the aneurysm sac
- ☐   E   usually starts at the level of the diaphragm

45 Rib tumours

☐ A are usually benign
☐ B are frequently due to symptomless secondaries
☐ C may be caused by multiple myeloma
☐ D should be removed surgically if benign
☐ E may result in pathological fracture

46 Injuries that are associated with nerve damage include

☐ A anterior dislocation of the shoulder
☐ B fracture of the shaft of the tibia
☐ C posterior fracture dislocation of the hip
☐ D fracture of the radial shaft
☐ E fracture of the clavicle

47 An arteriovenous fistula

☐ A may increase the pulse pressure
☐ B increases cardiac output
☐ C can cause distal ulceration
☐ D reduces central venous pressure
☐ E if congenital reduces growth in an affected limb

48 A patient with a 36 hour history of vomiting from a pyloric stenosis will

☐ A have a raised haematocrit (packed cell volume)
☐ B have increased urinary bicarbonate
☐ C have a low plasma pH
☐ D be hypokalaemic
☐ E be hyperchloraemic

49   Recognized features of salpingitis include

☐   A   colicky abdominal pain
☐   B   central abdominal pain
☐   C   pain referred to the umbilicus
☐   D   pain on sexual intercourse
☐   E   a presentation that is similar to that of ectopic pregnancy

50   Hyperplastic vulval dystrophy

☐   A   may be premalignant
☐   B   is a histological diagnosis
☐   C   is a feature of Paget's disease of the skin
☐   D   is also called senile dystrophy
☐   E   is untreatable

51   Dysfunctional uterine bleeding

☐   A   frequently affects the length of the menstrual cycle
☐   B   may be due to uterine fibroids
☐   C   is often associated with coagulation defects
☐   D   is treatable by dilatation and curettage
☐   E   frequently presents as oligomenorrhoea

52   At 28 weeks' gestation the management of premature rupture of the membranes includes

☐   A   a speculum examination
☐   B   a digital vaginal examination
☐   C   Caesarian section
☐   D   corticosteroids
☐   E   sympathomimetics

53 Secreting ovarian tumours produce

- ☐ A vasopressin
- ☐ B thyroxine
- ☐ C oestrogens
- ☐ D androgens
- ☐ E gonadotrophins

54 Recognized features of polycystic ovarian disease include

- ☐ A increased levels of LH
- ☐ B decreased levels of oestradiol
- ☐ C increased levels of testosterone
- ☐ D increased sex hormone binding globulin
- ☐ E ovarian cysts with reduced ovarian stroma

55 Recognized causes of postpartum haemorrhage include

- ☐ A halothane anaesthesia
- ☐ B retained placenta
- ☐ C multiple pregnancy
- ☐ D polyhydramnios
- ☐ E rhesus incompatibility

56 Recognized features of breech presentation include

- ☐ A 30% incidence at 34 weeks
- ☐ B premature labour
- ☐ C an extended breech, which is also known as a complete breech
- ☐ D cord prolapse in footling presentation
- ☐ E delivery by Caesarean section in most cases

57 Recognized causes of postmenopausal bleeding include

☐ A papilloma of the bladder
☐ B senile vaginitis
☐ C urethral carbuncle
☐ D carcinoma of the uterus
☐ E endometriosis

58 Characteristic features of endometriosis include

☐ A colicky abdominal pain
☐ B involvement of various organs
☐ C more severe pain a few days after menstruation
☐ D mittelschmerz
☐ E appendicitis

59 Characteristic clinical features of salpingitis are

☐ A onset in late teens
☐ B occurrence after childbirth
☐ C increased incidence with pregnancy
☐ D mycoplasma as the most common infecting organism
☐ E that although both tubes may be affected, only one tube is usually
      involved

60 Characteristic features of intramural fibroids include

☐ A anaemia
☐ B urinary stress incontinence
☐ C subfertility
☐ D postmenopausal bleeding
☐ E torsion

END OF EXAM 4

Go over your answers until your time is up. Answers and teaching notes are
on page 114.

60 Questions: time allowed 1½ hours.
Mark your answers with a tick (True) or a cross (False) in the box provided.
Leave the box blank for 'Don't know'.

1   The following complaints are commonly psychogenic:

☐ A exhaustion
☐ B impotence
☐ C inability to take a deep enough breath
☐ D left inframammary pain
☐ E seeing coloured haloes around lights

2   Recognized complications of acute myocardial infarction include

☐ A papillary muscle rupture
☐ B pericarditis
☐ C profound electrolyte imbalance
☐ D pneumonia
☐ E atrial fibrillation

3   Candidiasis is associated with

☐ A immunosuppression
☐ B diabetes mellitus
☐ C treatment with ampicillin
☐ D pregnancy
☐ E advanced age

4   The following are associated with emphysema

☐ A onset between 30 and 40 years of age
☐ B smoking and air pollution
☐ C barrel chest
☐ D well built appearance
☐ E cyanosis

5 **In the treatment of acidophil adenomas**

☐ A operation is rarely required
☐ B operation carries high risks
☐ C radiotherapy is ineffective
☐ D radium implants may be helpful
☐ E fatty degeneration of the heart may be reversed by hormonal manipulation

6 **The following are recognized unwanted side effects of the drugs named:**

☐ A hyperthyroidism – amiodarone
☐ B pseudomembranous colitis – vancomycin
☐ C pruritus – cholestyramine
☐ D dilutional hyponatraemia – demeclocycline
☐ E impotence – bendrofluazide

7 **Recognized side effects of broad spectrum antibiotics include**

☐ A diarrhoea
☐ B fulminant enterocolitis
☐ C oesophageal moniliasis
☐ D thrombocytopenia
☐ E iron deficiency anaemia

8 **Recognized features of multiple myeloma include**

☐ A chronic renal failure
☐ B spastic paraplegia
☐ C polycythaemia
☐ D raised serum gamma globulin
☐ E raised serum acid phosphatase

9   Hyperosmolar non-ketotic diabetes

- [ ] A should be treated with molar NaCl solution
- [ ] B should be treated with molar HCO_3 solution
- [ ] C should be treated with insulin
- [ ] D is found in juvenile diabetes mellitus
- [ ] E is difficult to treat

10   Characteristic features of bronchiectasis include

- [ ] A cough
- [ ] B blood stained sputum
- [ ] C malaise
- [ ] D clubbing
- [ ] E cerebral abscess

11   Recognized causes of homonymous hemianopia include

- [ ] A pituitary tumour
- [ ] B occipital tumour
- [ ] C retrobulbar neuritis
- [ ] D cerebral abscess
- [ ] E head injury

12   Depressed patients may show

- [ ] A agitation
- [ ] B poor concentration
- [ ] C hallucination
- [ ] D weight loss
- [ ] E decreased facial expression

13 Clinical manifestations of a meningioma compressing the spinal cord include

☐ A urinary incontinence
☐ B loss of sensation and temperature below the level of the lesion
☐ C loss of touch below the level of the lesion
☐ D spastic weakness of the muscles below the level of the lesion
☐ E loss of tendon reflexes

14 Features suggestive of combined mitral stenosis and incompetence rather than isolated mitral stenosis include

☐ A increased intensity of the first heart sound
☐ B left ventricular hypertrophy
☐ C left atrial hypertrophy
☐ D pulmonary hypertension
☐ E a loud opening snap

15 Recognized causes of unilateral blindness include

☐ A multiple sclerosis
☐ B lesions of the optic tract
☐ C lesions of the occipital lobe
☐ D olfactory groove meningiomas
☐ E lesions of the optic chiasm

16 In pseudobulbar palsy

☐ A there is fasciculation of the tongue
☐ B there is a bilateral lesion
☐ C inhalation pneumonia is common
☐ D in most patients there is a past history of hemiplegia
☐ E the lesion may be situated in the bulbar nuclei

17 The following occur more frequently in Crohn's disease than in ulcerative colitis:

☐ A transmural involvement of the bowel wall
☐ B rectal sparing
☐ C toxic dilatation of the colon
☐ D malignancy
☐ E gallstones

18 Causes of weakness of distal musculature include

☐ A chronic alcoholic intoxication
☐ B vinca alkaloids
☐ C dystrophia myotonica
☐ D thrombosis of the middle cerebral artery
☐ E hereditary mixed sensori-motor neuropathy

19 Malabsorption is a recognized feature of

☐ A Crohn's disease
☐ B multiple jejunal diverticulae
☐ C ulcerative colitis
☐ D intestinal polyposis
☐ E neomycin therapy

20 The following cause peripheral blood lymphocytosis:

☐ A systemic lupus erythematosus
☐ B whooping cough
☐ C toxoplasmosis
☐ D leptospirosis
☐ E whole body irradiation

21 Recognized features of systemic lupus erythematosus include

☐ A eosinophilia
☐ B peripheral arthropathy
☐ C splenomegaly
☐ D pericarditis
☐ E light sensitivity of the skin

22 Cyanosis may be a feature of the following:

☐ A tetralogy of Fallot
☐ B uncomplicated patent ductus arteriosus
☐ C coarctation of the aorta
☐ D ventricular septal defect
☐ E atrial septal defect

23 Trachoma

☐ A is caused by *Chlamydia*
☐ B is spread by direct transfer
☐ C is spread by infected meat
☐ D affects more than 10 million people worldwide
☐ E can be treated with tetracycline

24 Hydatid disease

☐ A occurs in the liver in 75% of cases
☐ B may be transmitted by foxes
☐ C is associated with sheep offal
☐ D can be passed on through contaminated meat
☐ E is especially common in Wales

25 Characteristic features of rheumatoid arthritis include

☐ A asymmetrical involvement of small joints
☐ B morning stiffness
☐ C afternoon fatigue
☐ D onset between the ages of 35 and 45
☐ E equal sex incidence

26 The following cause wasting of the muscles of the hand:

☐ A motor neurone disease
☐ B bronchial carcinoma
☐ C carpal tunnel syndrome
☐ D syringomyelia
☐ E Friedreich's ataxia

27 Characteristic features of a mole undergoing malignant change include

☐ A itching
☐ B bleeding
☐ C occurrence in a child
☐ D increasing pallor of the mole
☐ E superficial spread

28 In Parkinson's disease

☐ A the concentration of dopamine in the substantia nigra is decreased
☐ B the onset of symptoms is typically before the age of 40
☐ C there is characteristically a positive family history
☐ D ankle clonus is often present
☐ E chlorpromazine will significantly reduce the tremor

29 The facial nerve

☐ A is the motor supply for the face
☐ B is the sensory supply for the face
☐ C is the motor supply for the muscles of mastication
☐ D may be involved in parotid swelling
☐ E is affected in Bell's palsy

30 Blood glucose is increased by

☐ A adrenaline
☐ B glucagon
☐ C growth hormone
☐ D aldosterone
☐ E sulphonyl urea derivatives

31 Factors predisposing to the development of respiratory distress syndrome in the newborn include

☐ A maternal toxaemia
☐ B maternal diabetes
☐ C prematurity
☐ D perinatal asphyxia
☐ E maternal heroin addiction

32 Supracondylar fracture of the humerus in children

☐ A is a greenstick fracture in 50% of cases
☐ B is most commonly caused by a fall on the outstretched hand with the elbow slightly flexed
☐ C may be complicated by acute compartment syndrome
☐ D may damage the radial nerve but this requires expectant treatment only
☐ E typically unites in 3 to 4 weeks

33 Acute osteomyelitis in children

☐ A can be confirmed in early stages by radiological diagnosis
☐ B usually affects the diaphysis of the long bones
☐ C is most often caused by *Staphylococcus*
☐ D requires systemic antibiotic therapy for at least 3 weeks
☐ E is associated with a normal erythrocyte sedimentation rate in most children

34 The femoral triangle

☐ A is bounded by the medial border of adductor magnus and lateral border of sartorius
☐ B is bounded by the lateral border of adductor longus and the medial border of sartorius
☐ C has the lacunar ligament as a boundary
☐ D contains the femoral vein, artery and nerve all of which lie within the femoral sheath
☐ E has in its floor the pectineus muscle

35 A groin hernia

☐ A is most commonly an inguinal hernia
☐ B in young men is usually a direct hernia caused by lifting weights
☐ C in women is usually a femoral hernia
☐ D may contain bladder
☐ E may be repaired under local anaesthetic

36 Buerger's disease

☐ A is thought to be independent from smoking
☐ B is more common in women
☐ C affects the iliac arteries most commonly
☐ D is usually amenable to bypass surgery
☐ E is common in the elderly

37 Hashimoto's thyroiditis

- ☐ A is more common in men
- ☐ B usually occurs between the age of 30 and 50
- ☐ C may produce dysphagia
- ☐ D is characterized by an early onset of hypothyroidism
- ☐ E is usually associated with increased thyroid microsomal antibodies

38 Lower limb ulceration

- ☐ A may result from bed rest
- ☐ B is often caused by varicose veins
- ☐ C requires compression bandaging if arterial in origin
- ☐ D may follow deep vein thrombosis
- ☐ E may be associated with rest pain

39 A strangulated hernia

- ☐ A is tense
- ☐ B is tender
- ☐ C is resonant on percussion
- ☐ D has an expansile cough impulse
- ☐ E may contain the greater omentum

40 The following statements are true of ulceration:

- ☐ A peptic ulceration does not occur in the jejunum
- ☐ B neuropathic ulcers are common in patients with diabetes mellitus
- ☐ C leg ulcers may occur with hypersplenism
- ☐ D rodent ulcers only occur on the face
- ☐ E squamous cell carcinoma may arise in a rodent ulcer

41 Distension of the gallbladder is associated with carcinoma of the

☐ A ampulla of Vater
☐ B hepatic ducts
☐ C duodenum
☐ D common bile duct
☐ E head of pancreas

42 A 2 cm swelling in the neck at the junction of the upper and middle thirds of the right sternomastoid muscle

☐ A if fluctuant, is likely to be due to tuberculosis
☐ B if rubbery, could be due to Hodgkin's disease
☐ C if associated with dysphagia, is probably a pharyngeal pouch
☐ D if pulsatile, requires urgent exploration
☐ E if due to a branchial cyst, is self limiting and needs no further treatment

43 Carcinoma of the salivary glands

☐ A may cause a facial nerve palsy
☐ B rarely involves the parotid
☐ C commonly leads to ulceration of the overlying skin
☐ D usually occurs in patients over the age of 50
☐ E carries a poor prognosis

44 Acute otitis media

☐ A is frequently bilateral
☐ B is commonest in old age
☐ C usually results from infection via the pharyngo-tympanic (Eustachian) tube
☐ D frequently involves the mastoid ear cells
☐ E can result from diving

45 The following are indications for surgery (not simple suturing) in head injury

- ☐ A scalp lacerations
- ☐ B depressed skull fracture over the sagittal sinus
- ☐ C depressed skull fracture over the motor cortex
- ☐ D compound fracture
- ☐ E CSF rhinorrhoea for more than 10 days

46 In the management of perforated acute gastroduodenal ulceration

- ☐ A simple closure is the treatment of choice
- ☐ B simple closure is usually followed by a more definitive surgical procedure
- ☐ C gastric outlet obstruction is a contraindication to simple closure
- ☐ D the main disadvantage of conservative management is possible misdiagnosis
- ☐ E Ramstedt's pyloromyotomy may be required

47 Pain on defaecation is characteristic of

- ☐ A rectal carcinoma
- ☐ B pilonidal sinus
- ☐ C fissure *in ano*
- ☐ D haemorrhoids
- ☐ E fistula *in ano*

48 Characteristic features of Erbs–Duchenne (upper brachial plexus) injury include:

- ☐ A involvement of C7 and C8 roots
- ☐ B no associated sensory deficit
- ☐ C internal rotation of the arm
- ☐ D arthrodesis of the shoulder joint as a useful therapeutic procedure
- ☐ E syphilis as an underlying cause

49 The association of hypertension, albuminuria and oedema in pregnancy suggests

☐ A threatened abortion
☐ B ruptured ectopic pregnancy
☐ C incomplete abortion
☐ D hydatidiform mole
☐ E pre-eclampsia

50 An abnormally high level of alpha-fetoprotein in the liquor amnii may indicate

☐ A an open neural tube defect of the foetus
☐ B rhesus isoimmunisation
☐ C foetal growth retardation
☐ D twin pregnancy
☐ E pre-eclampsia

51 Recognized causes of postpartum shock without excessive blood loss include

☐ A inversion of the uterus
☐ B accidental intravenous administration of ergometrine
☐ C rupture of the uterus
☐ D paravaginal haematoma
☐ E a third degree tear

52 Excessive sickness in pregnancy

☐ A is associated with an increase in circulating pituitary gonadotrophins
☐ B is less common in pregnancy complicated by hydatidiform mole
☐ C tends to be more severe in twin pregnancy
☐ D responds to admission to hospital
☐ E may result in liver failure

53 Mild atypicalities in a cervical smear may be due to

☐ A cervical dysplasia
☐ B a cervical erosion
☐ C *Trichomonas vaginalis* infection
☐ D *Candida albicans* infection
☐ E pregnancy

54 Before forceps are applied the following conditions must be met:

☐ A full dilatation of the cervix
☐ B occipito-anterior position of the vertex
☐ C the bladder must be empty
☐ D uterine contractions should not be present
☐ E the forewaters should be ruptured

55 The following are significant adverse associations of combined oestrogen progesterone oral contraceptives:

☐ A migraine headaches
☐ B frequency of micturition
☐ C depression
☐ D loss of libido
☐ E hair loss

56 On day 7 of the menstrual cycle as compared with day 21

☐ A there is a lower progesterone concentration
☐ B there is a lower body temperature
☐ C there are more developing follicles
☐ D the endometrium is thicker
☐ E a smear of cervical mucus gives a fern-like pattern

57 Trichomonas vaginitis

☐ A is caused by a yeast like organism
☐ B is the most common form of vaginitis
☐ C causes a frothy discharge
☐ D is not associated with pruritus
☐ E responds well to metronidazole by mouth

58 The following changes in blood pressure control have occurred by the second trimester of normal pregnancy:

☐ A peripheral vascular resistance is increased
☐ B plasma renin activity is decreased
☐ C cardiac output is unchanged
☐ D aldosterone excretion is increased
☐ E myocardial contractility is increased

59 The following renal changes are typical of normal pregnancy:

☐ A increased glomerular filtration rate
☐ B decreased excretion of urate
☐ C decreased excretion of folate
☐ D increased excretion of glucose
☐ E ureteric dilatation

60 In the management of pregnancy in a diabetic woman

☐ A admission to hospital for the last trimester is essential
☐ B routine delivery before 38 weeks is advisable
☐ C delivery should be by the vaginal route if possible
☐ D purified or human insulin is preferable to crude bovine or porcine preparations
☐ E monitoring of urinary glucose is unnecessary

END OF EXAM 5
Go over your answers until your time is up. Answers and teaching notes are on page 127.

ANSWERS AND TEACHING NOTES

ANSWERS TO PRACTICE EXAM 1

The correct answer options are given against each question.

1   D E

Dysmetria is the inability to arrest a muscular movement at the desired point. It is a specific sign of cerebellar dysfunction and is therefore seen in Friedreich's ataxia which is a spinocerebellar degenerative disorder, but not in the extra-pyramidal movement disorders.

2   C E

Penicillamine can cause a drug-induced lupus nephritis, and gold causes a membranous glomerulonephritis. Prednisolone is often used for the treatment of nephrotic syndrome.

3   A C D E

Peripheral lymphadenopathy occurs in sarcoidosis and the histology can be diagnostic, showing non-caseating granulomata. Bronchial lavage is lymphocytic but this is not specific. Skeletal sarcoidosis occurs in 3–9% of patients and small bone cysts will be seen on X-rays of the hands and feet. 70% of these patients will also have abnormal chest X-rays and skin involvement. A negative Mantoux is found in 64% of patients with the disease, and in association with a raised serum angiotensin converting enzyme this finding becomes very suggestive of sarcoidosis. Kveim test involves the intradermal injection of material from validated human sarcoid spleen or lymph node, followed by biopsy at 6 weeks. If positive it is specific but the test is not sensitive.

4   A B

Diuretics deplete the vascular compartment causing activation of the renin-angiotensin-aldosterone system. They increase renal potassium loss. Thiazides are as effective in small as in large doses. Loop diuretics need be given in large doses only in the presence of renal impairment.

5   B D

Folate deficiency causes a megaloblastic anaemia and hypersegmentation of neutrophil nuclei ('right shift'). When severe, extramedullary haemato-poiesis gives rise to a leuko-erythroblastic blood film. Unlike Vitamin B12 deficiency there are no neurological complications. Folate deficiency has no effect on absorption of fats or on iron-binding capacity.

6 A B D E

Diabetes, myxoedema, nephrotic syndrome and oestrogens all cause hypercholesterolaemia. Other secondary causes include alcohol, cholestasis, chronic renal failure and myeloma.

7 A E

Travellers' diarrhoea is usually caused by enterotoxigenic strains of *Escherichia coli* (ETEC). It causes a profuse watery diarrhoea lasting 1 to 3 days. Mild opiates such as diphenoxylate hydrochloride ('Lomotil') are used as anti-motility agents. Persistent mild diarrhoea is most likely to be due to transient lactase deficiency. Amoebic infection causes dysentery, in which the diarrhoea is bloody.

8 A B C

Vitamin B12 deficiency resulting in anaemia is macrocytic. The absorption of this vitamin depends on gastric secretion of intrinsic factor (IF), which binds it. As the complex travels through the small bowel it is susceptible to breakdown by bacteria. Such bacterial overgrowth occurs when a blind-ending loop has been fashioned (as it is in Bilroth II gastrectomies). The IF-B12 complex is absorbed at the terminal ileum, except in the presence of a Crohn's terminal ileitis. Crohn's disease, unlike ulcerative colitis, can affect the small bowel, and therefore can cause folate malabsorption, another cause of macrocytic anaemia.

9 A B D

Hypokalaemia is associated with proton (hydrogen ion) depletion due to altered handling at the cell membrane and the renal tubule. It causes flattening of T waves (remember: 'no pot, no T') and appearance of U waves on the ECG. It can cause, but is not a result of, nephrogenic diabetes insipidus. Digoxin toxicity, in particular arrhythmias, can be exacerbated by hypokalaemia.

10 A B

Eosinophilia is most commonly a result of metazoan infestation. *Toxoplasma* is a genus of protozoans. It is also a feature of Hodgkin's lymphoma, asthma, allergic bronchopulmonary aspergillosis, Churg Strauss syndrome, polyarteritis nodosa, pulmonary eosinophilia and Loeffler's endocarditis.

11 A B D E

Urinary tract infection is commoner in women due to greater urethral reflux and vaginal colonisation with bacteria. Urinary counts of more than

10^5 bacteria per ml are considered significant. Suitable blind first-line therapy would include trimethoprim and amoxycillin and the advice to drink plenty of fluid.

12 A B C D
Psoriasis is associated with large joint oligoarthritis, sacroiliitis, assymetrical small joint arthritis with distal interphalangeal joint involvement and symmetrical polyarthritis with a rheumatoid-type distribution. Severe peripheral joint destruction is known as arthritis mutilans. Brucellosis is associated with a mono- or oligo-arthritis, which can be infective or reactive. Acute sarcoidosis presenting as erythema nodosum and bilateral hilar lymphadenopathy frequently includes a polyarthritis with minimal joint swelling that resolves in a few weeks. Rarely, the chronic form of the disease manifests itself as a destructive oligoarthritis. Amyloid arthropathy involves many joints and often includes carpal tunnel syndrome. Hyperlipidaemia can present with tendon xanthomata and if there is associated joint pain, can be mistaken for nodular rheumatoid arthritis. A true arthropathy, however, does not occur.

13 D
Vitamin B12 can be radiolabelled using cobalt. After saturating the body's binding sites with a large parenteral dose of unlabelled vitamin, a labelled dose is administered by mouth. Any that is absorbed will be excreted in the urine and can be measured. If a failure to absorb the vitamin is corrected by giving a simultaneous dose of intrinsic factor, the diagnosis is pernicious anaemia. This test helps to distinguish the different causes of vitamin B12 deficiency.

14 C D
Propranolol is the beta-blocker most commonly used in the prophylaxis of migraine. Pizotifen is a histamine and 5-hydroxytryptamine antagonist. Clonidine has been tried and found to be ineffective. Ergotamine is used in the acute attack and carbamazepine is used in the treatment of trigeminal neuralgia.

15 B C D
Acanthosis nigricans is a hyperpigmentation of the skin in the flexures often associated with intra-abdominal adenocarcinoma, but not with cutaneous malignancy. Leucoplakia, solar keratosis and Bowen's disease can all herald the appearence of squamous carcinoma of the skin. Squamous papilloma is a benign condition.

16 B C D

Enlargement of cardiac size on X-ray occurs when there is left ventricular dilatation or fluid within the pericardial sac. Mitral stenosis causes left atrial enlargement and while the cardiac silhouette is characteristically altered, its overall size is not.

17 A B C D E

Alcohol abuse and vomiting can both cause aspiration and subsequent lung collapse. In chronic bronchitis and asthma there is mucus plugging of bronchioles and distal collapse. Any impedance to large tidal volume respiration can cause small areas of collapse. Atelectatic areas act as foci for the development of pneumonia.

18 A B C E

In anorexia nervosa, pituitary gonadotrophin hyposecretion leads to amenorrhoea. Lassitude is often a feature and the development of lanugo hair is characteristic. It is a disease predominantly of young women and is associated with bulimia in which self-induced vomiting can give rise to hypokalaemia and pitting of the teeth by gastric acid.

19 A B E

Raised intracranial pressure causes a headache, particularly after lying down, coughing or straining. Visual obscurations and a reduction in conscious level ensue. Third nerve palsy is caused by pressure on the nerve as the uncus of the temporal lobe herniates below the tentorium cerebelli. This causes mydriasis, ophthalmoplegia and complete ptosis. Sixth nerve palsies can also occur. Convulsions can indicate the presence of an underlying space-occupying lesion in a patient with raised intracranial pressure.

20 B D E

Congenital hypothyroidism results in intellectual retardation but no brain hypoplasia. Early replacement therapy gives excellent results and all infants in the UK are screened. Other clinical features include constipation, poor feeding, pot belly and coarse facial features with macroglossia. Hypothyroidism is most commonly due to autoimmune disease of the thyroid gland, but pituitary failure is another important cause.

21 A B C E

Aspirin poisoning causes a variety of acid-base disturbances. As an acid it can cause a metabolic acidosis, but since it causes vomiting, loss of gastric acid and metabolic alkalosis can ensue. Brain stem effects include respiratory stimulation resulting in hyperventilation and respiratory alkalosis, and coma with subsequent hypoventilation and respiratory acidosis. Lavage, activated charcoal and aggressive rehydration with supportive therapy are the mainstays of treatment. Because of gastric atony, lavage may be helpful up to 24 hours following ingestion. Severe cases respond to haemofiltration.

22 A D E

The predominant finding in the thalassaemias is the failure to manufacture haemoglobin. Red cells are defective and subject to extravascular haemolysis, causing hyperbilirubinaemia and bile pigment gall stones. There is expansion of the haematopoietic tisssues with hepatosplenomegaly and characteristic skull deformities. Treatment is with transfusion of normal red cells and iron overload can cause cardiomyopathy, hepatic and multiple endocrine failure, as well as increased skin pigmentation.

23 A B C D E

Adult polycystic kidney disease is inherited in an autosomal dominant fashion. It is associated with intracranial berry aneurysms, as well as hepatic, pancreatic, ovarian, and pneumonic cysts. It can present with loin pain due to haemorrhage or infection in a cyst, the kidneys are enlarged and chronic renal failure with hypertension develops. Renal stones occur in 10% of patients with polycystic kidneys. Renal and transitional cell carcinoma are both seen in affected kidneys.

24 A C D E

Bacterial meningitis results in a polymorph-predominant pleocytosis in the CSF. With pneumococcal meningitis, a mixed polymorph-lymphocyte population of cells is often seen. An urgent Gram stain should always be done to look for causative organisms. Protein is usually raised and glucose reduced.

25 A B C

Chronic otitis media has become a rarer cause of facial palsy since the introduction of antibiotics. Any surgical procedure along the route of the nerve can damage it. The commonest causes of facial nerve palsy are Bell's palsy (idiopathic) and Ramsay Hunt syndrome (geniculate Herpes zoster reactivation).

26 B C E

Finger clubbing is seen in carcinomatous and suppurative diseases of the lung and pleura, interstitial lung diseases, cyanotic congenital heart disease and subacute bacterial endocarditis. Rarer causes are congenital clubbing, liver cirrhosis and inflammatory bowel disease.

27 B C

The procedure in cardiac arrest is to establish airway patency and institute artificial ventilation first, then to perform cardiac massage. The aim is to oxygenate the brain until the end of the arrest. The highest concentration of oxygen that can be given should therefore be used. Intravenous adrenaline should be administered regularly as the vasoconstriction maintains venous return and cardiac filling. Intracardiac adrenaline given into the cardiac cavity can be used if intravenous adrenaline has been unsuccessful. Ventricular tachyarrhythmias can be terminated with unsynchronated DC shock.

28 C E

Non-Hodgkin's lymphomata of the B-cell lineage can produce a para-protein of monoclonal immunoglobulin. The production of autoantibodies and autoimmune haemolytic anaemia may be seen in lymphoma. Immuno-deficiency is a result of the disease or of the treatment and causes opportunistic infections. Extra-dural deposits in the spinal canal cause acute paraplegia.

29 A B D

Phenobarbitone and baclofen are capable of precipitating acute attacks of porphyria, which can manifest itself as an acute motor neuropathy. Phenytoin-induced peripheral neuropathy is rare.

30 C

Smallpox, rubella, Sabin and yellow fever vaccines are live but only the latter is cultivated in chick embryos. Salk vaccine is inactivated.

31 B C

Fixation is limited to a 90° angle by 4 weeks of age. At 8 weeks a dangling toy is followed from side to a point just past the midline and from side to side i.e. an arc of 180° by 12 weeks. At this age vertical orientation is developing. By 6 weeks most infants are smiling in response to being looked at or spoken to by a parent. With ventral suspension the head is held in the same plane as the body by 8 weeks. Only by 20 weeks is full head control gained. By 12 weeks the infant will start to coo and make nosies.

32 D E

Both conditions are associated with arthralgia and joint swelling and both may have casts within the urine. Abdominal pain is a common feature of Henoch–Schönlein purpura. Intussusception is more common in Henoch–Schönlein and may present in this fashion. Melaena occurs with Henoch–Schönlein purpura due to mucosal ulceration and bleeding from the intestinal wall.

33 A B C

Rebound tenderness may be a feature of peritonism seen in acute appendicitis. Classically the pain commences as being periumbilical and then descends to McBurney's point. A raised number of white cells in the urine suggests a urinary tract infection; however appendicitis may give rise to a similar number of white cells hence it cannot be excluded. Chest infections may be evidenced by bronchial breathing. This and severe diarrhoea may both present with abdominal pain.

34 A C

The risk of extradural haematoma or spinal haemorrhage outweighs the possible benefits of this technique in patients who are anticoagulated. Six hours' preoperative starvation is thought to be adequate for most operations including gastric surgery which usually requires relaxation to enable access. A *double* lumen tube is used to enable partial collapse of a lung on the operated side of the chest. (A triple lumen tube usually refers to a Sengstaken tube for oesophageal varices.) A Swan Ganz catheter is a flotation occlusion catheter which is used to measure the wedge pressure in a branch of the pulmonary *artery* (veins have tributaries).

35 A B C E

Acute endocarditis, cyanotic congenital heart disease and bronchiectasis all increase the risk of haematogenous spread of infection to the brain whereas otitis media causes infection by direct spread.

36 A B C D

Food poisoning; for example *Bacillus cereus* from reheating rice; can cause symptoms suggestive of appendicitis. Perforated peptic ulcer can cause central or epigastric pain which spreads down the right paracolic gutter to the right iliac fossa causing diagnostic difficulty. Crohn's disease commonly affects the ileocaecal region, although a somewhat longer history and systemic symptoms often suggest the diagnosis. Painful ovulation in the middle ('mittel' in German) of the cycle particularly in young girls is a well recognized cause of presentation which may be mistaken for appendicitis.

37 A B D
Diarrhoea is a common side effect of antibiotics due an alteration in faecal flora. In pseudomembranous colitis there is overgrowth of *Clostridium difficile* causing a life threatening illness. Fungal infection tends to result from prolonged use of antibiotics not prophylaxis and does not affect the colon (usually oral and occasionally oesophageal). Thrombocytopenia is a well recognized side effect of many antibiotics. Iron deficiency anaemia is usually due to blood loss (iron stores would negate any effect on iron absorption).

38 A C E
Cleft palate and other maxillofacial deformities predispose to middle ear problems. Non-suppurative (secretory) otitis media ('glue ear') is characterized by a sterile middle ear infection which varies in consistency from thin to viscid. The slow accumulation of fluid often manifests itself in behavioural or learning difficulties due to painless loss of hearing. Facial palsy is a complication of acute suppurative otitis media.

39 B C D E
A 'blow out' characteristically occurs on the 4th postoperative day. Poor mixing of food and enzymes, reduced production and inactivation of pancreatic enzymes within the afferent loop, and jejunal atrophy may produce altered absorption of fats, vitamin D and calcium. Lag storage glycosuria (symptomless glycosuria) occurs when there is a rapid absorption of glucose above the renal threshold. Pulmonary tuberculosis is more common after gastric surgery and is thought to be due to reactivation of a latent focus associated with malnutrition.

40 D
Hypospadias is a relatively common congenital abnormality caused by a failure of fusion of the urethral folds with the ectodermal plate. It is usually treated at about the age of 2–3 years (to avoid missing school). The foreskin should be preserved for reconstructive surgery when it can be used as a skin flap. It is however often deformed ('hooded') and may be removed during definitive surgery. The advice not to perform circumcision in patients with hypospadias exhorts surgeons to think of the diagnosis before circumcision. The glandular variety of hypospadias is the most common and rarely requires surgery. Chordee (fibrous bands) cause the penis to bend ventrally (downwards).

41 B

Paget's disease like other breast cancers may rarely be bilateral. It is almost invariably (but not always!!) associated with an underlying ductal carcinoma of the breast. It is generally a disease of postmenopausal women. It has a good prognosis if treated by mastectomy. Histology shows the characteristic 'Pagetoid cells' which are large vacuolated cells with small deeply staining nucleoli.

42 A B C E

Oral contraceptives (perhaps especially the older high oestrogen content pills) are thought to increase the risk of gallstones. In at least 8% of postmortems in patients over the age of 50 there are 'silent' gallstones. Gallstone ileus is a rare but serious complication. Congenital spherocytosis and other haemolytic anaemias causing increased red cell turnover increase the risk of pigment gallstones but iron deficiency anaemia does not. Almost 90% of patients with carcinoma of the gallbladder have gallstones.

43 A B D

Hutchison's melanotic mole (lentigo maligna) is definitely a premalignant condition where the large facial mole undergoes central melanomatous change. Bowen's disease is an intradermal precancerous condition which appears as an area of brownish induration in the skin. Whereas lupus vulgaris predisposes to squamous cell tumours, lupus erythematosus (SLE) does not. Chronic leg ulcers particularly venous ulcers and those associated with osteomyelitis (Marjolin's ulcer) can develop squamous cell carcinoma. Acanthosis nigricans is a subcutaneous manifestation of a *visceral* malignancy.

44 A D E

Paralytic ileus (adynamic obstruction) is almost invariable after open abdominal surgery. It causes diffuse dilatation of the whole bowel and not just the ileum. In strangulation obstruction it is a late and serious development. Air in the peritoneal cavity indicates visceral perforation and is not a radiological sign of ileus (though it may commonly be seen postoperatively). Retroperitoneal injury may cause a prolonged ileus.

45 B D E

Actinomycosis is caused by an anaerobic Gram-positive branching filamentous organism (*Actinomyces israelii*) which produces a chronic indurating inflammation with sinuses in the facio-cervical (including the jaw), thoracic, hepatic and ileocaecal regions. It is usually sensitive to penicillin.

46 A B D

Plummer-Vinson (Paterson-Brown-Kelly) syndrome of iron deficiency anaemia and an oesophageal web causing dysphagia is a premalignant condition as is achalasia where prolonged stasis is thought to contribute to the mucosal changes. Reflux oesophagitis with the development of Barrett's oesophagitis (10% become malignant) accounts for up to 15% of cases of carcinoma of the oesophagus; a condition which is three times more common in men. Coeliac disease predisposes to small bowel lymphoma.

47 B E

Flail chest is the result of multiple rib fractures causing paradoxical chest movement apparent on clinical examination. The flail segment is sucked in during inspiration and pushed out during expiration. It is the result of massive blunt trauma and there is often an underlying haemopneumothorax. Significant shunting may occur and it is sometimes necessary to ventilate these patients; however, ventilation produces its own morbidity and if they can be managed with epidural or intercostal analgesia and physiotherapy this is preferable. Stabilization is rarely required.

48 C E

Dupuytren's contracture is a localized contracture of the palmar fascia, and characteristically affects the ring and little fingers. There is a familial predisposition; and it may be related to alcohol abuse or cirrhosis. Surgery can be very difficult and occasionally amputation is necessary.

49 A

Abortion becomes inevitable in *all* cases once the internal cervical os opens. This is associated with abdominal pain and increased vaginal bleeding. Excessive vaginal bleeding alone, however, does not always result in abortion. Once products of conception are expelled through the internal os, the situation is no longer 'inevitable' and is termed instead as 'complete' or 'incomplete' abortion, depending upon the degree of uterine emptying. The external cervical os remains partially open in many women after the first pregnancy and does not imply a poor outcome in cases of threatened abortion. Pregnancy tests often remain positive in women with inevitable abortion until the products of conception are completely expelled.

50 A B C D

Genito-urinary fistulae are a recognized complication of a) malignant disease, b) radiotherapy, c) surgical trauma, d) chronic inflammatory conditions, e) obstructed labour and difficult instrumental delivery. The basic mechanism here is tissue loss due to ischaemia, and local tissue destruction from acute penetrative injuries, chronic ulceration or malignant infiltration. Herpetic lesions are too superficial and transient for fistulae formation.

51 C

The precise amount of radiation that is harmful to the foetus is not known. However, it is estimated that radiation exposure of less that 0.5 Gy represents no measurable risk to the foetus in late pregnancy. As 0.5 Gy is about x100 the exposure received during an abdominal X-ray, the foetus should be safe from radiation damage if the mother requires an investigation of this nature in the third trimester. Congenital abnormalities are more reliably detected by high-resolution ultrasound scans. X-rays are only useful if ultrasound features are unclear in suspected skeletal abnormalities. Placental calcification is a non-specific change and is not indicative of placental ageing. Ultrasonic localization of the placenta is more reliable than radiography.

52 A C E

Pre-eclampsia and eclampsia occur more commonly in the first than in subsequent pregnancies. In multipara, pregnancy with a new partner increases the incidence to that of a first pregnancy. At present in the UK only 25% of eclamptic women present antenatally. The majority have convulsions in the immediate postpartum period. Cerebrovascular haemorrhages, oedema and ischaemia can cause coma and localising neurological deficits that are reversed gradually following delivery of the foetus and placenta. Any stimulus can precipitate a fit, hence efforts must be made to cut down external triggers. Patients however must be nursed in an adequately lit room to allow appropriate nursing and medical care. Hyperreflexia is a sign of imminent eclampsia and may also be elicited between recurrent fits in severe cases.

53 B C D E

Postpartum haemorrhage (PPH) is defined as blood loss in excess of 500 ml after delivery of the foetus. Antepartum haemorrhage from placental abruption and placenta praevia predisposes to PPH. Coagulation failure and/or a Couvelaire uterus resulting from placental abruption may prevent effective uterine contraction after childbirth. In placenta praevia, the lower uterine segment has fewer muscle fibres to contract down the open sinuses at the implantation site, resulting in greater blood loss. Overdistension of the uterus and the large placental bed in multiple pregnancies can cause PPH. Platelet deficiency states, e.g. idiopathic thrombocytopenia, predispose to PPH. Active management of the third stage of labour with oxytocic agents reduces blood loss considerably and is routinely practised in all maternity units in the UK.

54 A B C
Between 0.5–5% of pregnancies are associated with fibroids. The vast majority are asymptomatic. In some cases, fibroids may grow very rapidly in the second half of pregnancy, outstripping their blood supply. This leads to painful red degeneration (necrobiosis) of the central area of the fibroid. Abdominal pain may also result from torsion of pedunculated fibroids. Fibroids do not cause antepartum haemorrhage, but the abdominal pain resulting from the complications mentioned may be mistaken for pain from concealed placental abruption. Fibroids, however, predispose to postpartum haemorrhage by interfering with effective uterine contraction after delivery. Symptomatic fibroids in pregnancy should be managed medically except when pedunculated fibroids undergo torsion of a narrow pedicle that is easy to ligate and divide.

55 All false
Stress incontinence is caused by inadequate transmission of intra-abdominal pressure to the urethra. This may be associated with (but not caused by) loss of the urethrovesical angle or with cystourethrocele. Multiple sclerosis typically causes detrusor hyperreflexia or detrusor sphincter dyssynergia.

56 A B C E
Genital herpes caused by herpes simplex virus – 2, and less commonly herpes simplex virus – 1, can present as recurrent painful vulval ulcers. Most squamous cell carcinomas of the vulva appear as painful ulcers with irregular everted margins. Chancres are painless shallow ulcers typical of the first stage of syphilis. They usually affect the cervix, but may also occur on the labia. Atrophic vulvitis occurs after the menopause and is thought to be due to oestrogen deficiency. The skin becomes thin and shiny but ulceration is not a feature of this condition. Lymphogranuloma inguinale (venereum) caused by *Chlamydia trachomatis* presents as shallow labial ulcers which gradually deepen and extend. They heal gradually leaving irregular scars and 'windows' where tissue is destroyed.

57 A B C D

Human placental lactogen is a placental protein hormone produced by the syncitiotrophoblast. It is probably the main hormone ensuring an adequate supply of glucose to the foetus. Low levels of the hormone are associated with intra-uterine growth retardation (IUGR) and increased perinatal mortality. It is detectable in maternal serum from as early as the 8th week of pregnancy, and continues to rise in concentration as the pregnancy advances. It is responsible for the increased peripheral resistance to insulin seen in pregnancy.

58 A C D

Monilial infection is caused by a yeast-like fungus called *Candida* (monilia) *albicans*. It can cause intense vulval pruritus. Monilial mycelia can co-exist with the protozoan *Trichomonas vaginalis,* in the vagina. Both organisms produce a discharge which results in vulval pruritus and soreness. Monilial infection is treated with fungicides such as nystatin or clotrimazole. Antibiotics such as ampicillin predispose to monilial infection by altering the normal flora of commensals that usually hold the vaginal mycelia in check and prevent them from multiplying.

59 A B C

For the safe and effective application of forceps, the presenting part must be engaged and the presentation must be either vertex or face with the chin anterior. Forceps can also be applied to the after-coming head of a breech. Non-engagement in the second stage may be due to cephalopelvic disproportion, an absolute contraindication to the application of forceps. Prior emptying of the bladder avoids the risk of injuring it during forceps delivery. The application of forceps blades before full dilation of the cervix is difficult and requires greater traction to overcome resistance from the cervical rim. Considerable maternal tissue trauma may result from this. Uterine contractions are necessary to facilitate forceps delivery and should be stimulated with oxytocin infusion if required. Forceps may be used to deliver a non-viable foetus if the mother is unable to do so unaided.

60 C D

Secondary infertility is the term used when a couple have previously achieved at least one pregnancy, regardless of the outcome of that pregnancy. A variety of medical conditions may cause secondary infertility, but in a substantial minority (5–10%) the condition may remain unexplained. Secondary infertility may or may not be reversible depending upon the aetiological factors involved. Secondary syphilis is but one of many infections that can result in infertility.

ANSWERS TO PRACTICE EXAM 2

1   C E

An ejection mid-systolic murmur heard at the left sternal edge and accentuated by the Valsalva manoeuvre is characteristic of hypertrophic obstructive cardiomyopathy (HOCM). The fourth heart sound is an atrial sound and is therefore absent in atrial fibrillation. An atrial septal defect causes a wide, fixed-split second sound. A venous hum is a feature of auscultation in children. A persistent ductus causes a continuous 'machinery' murmur. Papillary muscle infarction is a complication of acute myocardial infarction and causes mitral regurgitation.

2   B E

Myotonic dystrophy has autosomal dominant inheritance. The chromosomal abnormality is an expansion of trinucleotide repeats. These can get longer in each generation, leading to the phenomenon of anticipation, where the disease becomes more severe in subsequent generations. Myotonia congenita has autosomal recessive and autosomal dominant forms. The latter is called Thomsen's disease. Gilbert's syndrome (intermittent hyperbilirubinaemia) is inherited in a non-Mendelian fashion. Nephrogenic diabetes insipidus is X-linked recessive. Tuberous sclerosis is usually inherited as an autosomal recessive.

3   A B C E

The alkaline phosphatase is raised in cholestasis and in situations of increased osteoclasis (bone resorption by osteoclasts), with increased bone remodelling by osteoblasts. In myeloma, there is little osteoblastic activity and therefore the alkaline phosphatase is normal. It may be raised, however, if there is liver infiltration.

4   B D E

A diagnosis of systemic lupus erythematosus is suggested by a non-erosive polyarthropathy, pleuropericarditis, photosensitive rash or livedo reticularis, alopecia, mouth ulcers, recurrent vascular thromboses or signs of neuropsychiatric or renal disease. Blood count may show anaemia, lymphopenia and/or thrombocytopenia.

5   B C D

Erythema nodosum is a painful nodular rash on the anterior shins. A rarer but more specific skin lesion seen in TB is erythema induratum (Bazin's disease). Primary tuberculosis can cause an allergic phlyctenicular conjunctivitis but this is rare. Renal tract TB causes haematuria. Erythema marginatum is seen only in acute rheumatic fever. Arachnodactyly is a feature of Marfan's syndrome.

6   **A B C D E**
Major incompatibility reactions cause acute intravascular haemolysis resulting in a rise in serum bilirubin and a depletion of haptoglobin. Free haemoglobin and methaemoglobin appear in the urine. Disseminated intravascular coagulation can ensue. Chest, lumbar or loin pain may occur with intravascular haemolysis. Cytokine release causes tachycardia, hypotension and rigors. Oliguria may result from prolonged hypotension.

7   **A B**
Miliary tuberculosis is an uncommon but often fatal complication of primary infection. Clinical features include fever, malaise, dyspnoea and hepatosplenomegaly. The presence of choroidal tubercles confirms the diagnosis. Chronic sarcoidosis commonly involves the spleen. Caisson's disease is otherwise known as decompression sickness. It is seen in divers who surface too quickly. Nitrogen bubbles appear in the blood and embolise to the joints, skin, lungs and central nervous system.

8   **C E**
The bleeding time is prolonged in thrombocytopenia or disorders of platelet function. In von Willebrand's disease, lack of von Willebrand factor impairs aggregation of platelets at sites of endothelial damage.

9   **A B D E**
Benzodiazepine overdose and other causes of brain stem respiratory depression cause hypoventilation and obtusion but not cough. Cough may be a feature of anxiety or nervousness. Any cause of bronchial or alveolar irritation will result in cough.

10   **A B D E**
Most inflammatory and autoimmune diseases are more common in women. HLA–B27 associated arthropathies and polyarteritis nodosa are exceptions. Congenital pyloric stenosis is more common in males. Coarctation of the aorta is twice as common in males as in females. Rheumatic mitral valve lesions are more commonly seen in females.

11   **B C D**
Melanosis coli is pigmentation of the colonic mucosa caused by long-

term purgative abuse. Familial adenomatous polyposis and inflammatory bowel disease predispose to adenocarcinoma of the bowel. Lichen sclerosus can presage squamous skin carcinoma. Peyronie's disease is a condition in which there is distortion and deviation of the penis caused by connective tissue plaque and may be associated with Dupuytren's contracture. It does not predispose to malignancy.

12 B D

True vertigo is caused by disease of the labyrinths and their brain stem connections. Mumps can cause an acute labyrinthitis. Syringobulbia is a pathological expansion of the fourth ventricle and acqueduct of Sylvius. It causes sensory loss on the head, sparing the face ('balaclava distribution'), vertigo and lower motor neurone lesions of the Xth, XIth and XIIth cranial nerves. Common causes of vertigo include benign positional nystagmus, Meniere's disease, cerebello-pontine angle tumours and vascular insufficiency in the distribution of the basilar artery. Quinine toxicity causes tinnitus ('cinchonism') but not vertigo.

13 C

Recent onset and the presence of a reduced level of consciousness or acute systemic illness suggest delirium rather than dementia. Sixth nerve palsy would only suggest an acute confusional state if it was of recent onset. Disorientation of time and place, with no further information regarding length of history, does not distinguish the two conditions.

14 A C D E

Purpura is a manifestation of haemostatic or vascular wall dysfunction. In scurvy there is dietary deficiency of vitamin C (ascorbic acid). Collagen synthesis is impaired and there is vascular breakdown leading characteristically to follicular haemorrhage. A streptococcal throat infection can lead to scarlet fever which results in an erythematous rash. However, immune mechanisms may result in a purpuric rash in streptococcal infections and in association with nephritis (e.g. Henoch–Schönlein purpura). Scurvy and cutaneous vasculitis are examples of non-thrombocytopenic purpura and are due to vessel-wall defects. Haemophilia results in easy bruising (echymoses) and bleeding into joints.

15 A B D

A patient with hypertension and different kidney sizes has renal artery stenosis until proven otherwise. Unilateral vesico-ureteric reflux could cause a chronic interstitial nephritis affecting one kidney as can any infection, including tuberculosis. It would not only be small but irregularly shaped with sub-cortical scarring. In polyarteritis nodosa, the kidneys are usually of normal size but microaneurysms may result in haemorrhage. Renal tumours result in an increase in renal size.

16 B D E

An extensor plantar response (Babinski's sign) and an absent ankle jerk are only seen together when there is both a corticospinal tract lesion and an afferent defect of the dorsal columns. The former occurs in general paresis of the insane (endarteritis and infarction of brain parenchyma) and the latter in tabes dorsalis (dysfunction of the dorsal columns of the spinal cord). The two occur together in taboparesis. These are both features of tertiary syphilis. Subacute combined degeneration of the cord is caused by vitamin B12 deficiency and is so called because it affects the dorsal columns and corticospinal tracts. Other conditions in which this occurs include syringomyelia and Friedreich's ataxia.

17 B C

Pure B-lymphocyte defects cause hypogammaglobulinaemia. One of the more well-defined primary forms is Bruton's which is X-linked recessive. Mild immunoglobulin deficiency may be sub-clinical and of variable inheritance but significant disease leads to recurrent and chronic suppurative infection. It is more common than T-cell disorders, some of which can be treated with thymic implants. Antibiotics are the mainstay of therapy for hypogammaglobulinaemia.

18 B C E

The intrinsic hand muscles are all supplied by the T1 nerve root via the ulnar nerve (except for the lateral two **L**umbricals, **O**ponens pollicis brevis, **A**bductor pollicis brevis and **F**lexor pollicis brevis; '**LOAF**') which are under median nerve control). Spread of apical lung carcinoma to affect the T1 nerve root is called a Pancoast tumour, but generalised muscle wasting may be seen as a non-metastatic manifestation of malignant disease. Motor neurone disease causes widespread lower motor neurone lesions with wasting and fasciculations. The wasting seen in rheumatoid arthritis is thought to be partly secondary to disuse.

19 A B C D E

Lithium causes nephrogenic diabetes insipidus (DI), as does hypokalaemia. Hypokalaemia causes tetany and in the context of hypertension and a proximal myopathy is likely to be caused by ectopic ACTH secretion. Carbamazepine has been used in the treatment of nephrogenic DI.

Bilateral hilar lymphadenopathy is a presentation of sarcoidosis which can cause nephrogenic DI secondary to hypercalcaemia and cranial DI as a result of infiltration of the posterior pituitary gland. The patient with anaemia, hypertension and hyperventilation induced by metabolic acidosis may have chronic renal failure, in which the kidneys' concentrating ability can be lost.

20 A C

Pulmonary oedema is a common complication of blood transfusion, which should be given with a loop diuretic in the presence of heart disease or in the elderly. Hypothermia only results from giving cool blood in massive transfusions. Millipore filters prevent leucocyte mediated febrile reactions. Packed cells have a life-time of 35 days after preparation as long as they are kept at 4°C. Once warmed they last for only 6 hours.

21 A C D

Horner's syndrome is partial ptosis, miosis and enophthalmos of one eye and anhydrosis of the face on the ipsilateral side. It is caused by interruption of the sympathetic innervation of the face, which descends through the medulla as far as T1 and exits with the nerve root to join the sympathetic chain. Fibres then ascend in nervous plexi close to the internal carotid artery. Common causes of Horner's syndrome include damage during surgery and direct (non-metastatic) infiltration by tumour (e.g. Pancoast tumour). Thrombosis of the posterior inferior cerebellar artery results in damage to the sympathetic pathways within the medulla (Wallenberg's syndrome). Syringomyelia may affect the sympathetic pathways in the cervical cord. Surgery for congenital heart disease may damage the recurrent laryngeal or phrenic nerves.

22 A B D

Scurvy is due to the dietary deficiency of vitamin C (ascorbic acid). Gingivitis leads to gum hyperplasia and bleeding. Follicular haemorrhage in the skin and subperiosteal haemorrhage is characteristic. A blue line along the gum is found in lead poisoning and a raw tongue is a manifestation of the glossitis seen in anaemia.

23 A B D

Ichthyosis is a skin disorder in which there is widespread scaling. The appearance is said to resemble fish scales. The vulgaris form is the commonest and is inherited in an autosomal dominant fashion. Typically there is sparing of the skin creases. Histology shows a decrease in the granular layer of the epidermis.

24   A B C D E
Dysphagia occurs in various contexts. Raynaud's phenomenon and oesophageal dysmotility form part of the CREST (Calcinosis, Raynaud's, Esophageal dysmotility, Sclerodactyly, Telangiectasia) syndrome (limited scleroderma). A fibrillating tongue is a sign of bulbar palsy which causes dysphagia, dysarthria and a bovine cough. It is often a feature of motor neurone disease. Long-standing iron deficiency anaemia causes koilonychia and an oesophageal web (Patterson–Brown–Kelly or Plummer–Vinson syndrome). Tylosis is a palmar and plantar skin thickening (hyperkeratosis) seen with carcinoma of the oesophagus. Immunosuppression can result in oesophageal candidiasis.

25   B D E
The hypotension of systemic sepsis is multifactorial. It is initiated by bacterial endotoxaemia and immune cell-mediated cytokine release. There is peripheral vasodilatation and myocardial depression. Increased capillary permeability leads to hypovolaemia. Cyanosis can be a result of increased physiological shunting through the lungs or Adult Respiratory Distress Syndrome (ARDS). The condition frequently results in multiorgan failure and death. Broad spectrum antibiotics should be given to treat the underlying cause and the results of blood cultures may be of help in directing subsequent treatment. Corticosteroid therapy may leave the patient more susceptible to infection.

26   A C D
A peaked 'p' wave taller than 3 mm is diagnostic of right atrial enlargement. Right atrial enlargement might occur as a result of tricuspid valve stenosis and pulmonary hypertension. Left atrial enlargement causes lengthening of the p wave form and a notched, bicuspid pattern in lead II and a biphasic pattern in lead V1 ('p mitrale').

27   A C D
Periorbital oedema is characteristic of nephrotic syndrome in children. Swelling around the eye may also be a feature of the vasculitic rash of dermatomyositis. Ophthalmic Graves' disease results in deposition of tissue with oedema behind the eye (resulting in proptosis) and in the periorbital tissues. Acute iritis causes conjunctival injection around the iris and iridospasm. The anterior chamber fills with inflammatory cells and appears cloudy. These cells can form a sediment known as a hypopyon. The skin around the eye in systemic sclerosis is usually tight, contributing to the characteristic mask-like facies.

28 A B C D E
The visual field loss in acromegaly is typically a bitemporal hemianopia. The characteristic appearance of patients with acromegaly includes sweaty, greasy skin, large tongue, prognathic jaw and spade-shaped hands. There is secondary hypertension and premature atherosclerosis in this condition. Both diabetes mellitus and osteoarthritis occur with increased frequency in acromegaly.

29 B C D E
Cholestasis and convulsions are rare. Common side-effects include dry mouth, blurred vision, urinary retention, constipation, drowsiness and impotence. Patients who have taken excessive amounts of tricyclic antidepressants should be monitored for arrhythmia.

30 A B C D
Noradrenaline has effects mainly at the alpha-adrenoceptor and less so at the beta$_1$-receptor. Peripheral vasoconstriction causes a rise in systemic vascular resistance and of blood pressure. Hepatic glycogenolysis is controlled by beta$_2$-receptor agonism.

31 A C D E
Hypoparathyroidism is not generally associated with growth retardation but pseudohypoparathyroidism is.

32 D E
Hyperbilirubinaemia is associated with athetoid cerebral palsy. Intracranial malignanies are very uncommon in presenting with cerebral palsy and a high stepping gait is more associated with sensory disturbance such as is seen in syphilis! There do appear to be some families with a congenital predisposition to developing cerebral spastic quadraplegia and the incidence is increased with multiple births, perhaps due to obstetric complications.

33 A B C E
Malignancy may present with failure to thrive and delay in bone age. More commonly therapies used in treating the malignancy may give rise to retarded bone age such as non-ionising radiation. Down's children have an increased incidence of atlanto-axial dislocation but not delayed bone age.

34 B D

Onychogryphosis is usually due to a fungal infection of the nail which occurs in the elderly. It is often symptomless but as the deformed nail enlarges it is liable to trauma and can become painful. It is not a manifestation of systemic disease.

35 B E

Large bowel obstruction is most commonly due to colonic carcinoma. Pseudo-obstruction (adynamic) is not uncommon in patients with systemic disease, usually due to drug side effects or electrolyte disturbances, such as hypokalaemia. Vomiting when present is faeculent and is a late sign.

36 C D

An inguinal hernia and a patent processus come through the internal ring and therefore one cannot 'get above' them. Tuberculous epididymo-orchitis produces a thickened caseous swelling which does not transilluminate.

37 C D

The commonest cause of bleeding remains peptic ulceration often associated with use of non-steroidal anti-inflammatory drugs (NSAIDs). A low initial haemoglobin is a positive risk factor for rebleeding as is a visible vessel on endoscopy. The morbidity and mortality in older patients is reduced if prompt surgery is performed at the time of the first rebleed. Haematemesis is more common in gastric ulcers (60%:40%), whereas melaena is more common in duodenal ulcers (40%:60%).

38 B C E

Aniline dye workers (not aniseed which is a food flavouring) were at risk of bladder cancer because of beta-naphthalene contamination of the dyestuff. Other high risk occupations include the rubber industry, gas workers and printing. A diverticulum is associated with urinary stasis and predisposes to both infection and squamous metaplasia which can lead, in 7–8% of patients to squamous carcinoma with a poor prognosis partly due to late presentation. Schistosomiasis (bilharzia), due to the helminths *Schistosoma haematobium*, *S. mansoni* and *S. japonicum* predisposes to squamous metaplasia and squamous cell carcinoma. Malaria does not cause bladder cancer. Transitional cell (urothelial) carcinoma is the commonest form of malignant tumour of the bladder (>90%).

39   B E

Klumpke's paralysis is a flaccid, lower brachial plexus injury (C8, T1), usually caused by a traction injury or fall with the limb in the abducted position or due to birth injury. All the small muscles of the hand are affected resulting in a claw hand from the unopposed action of the long flexors and extensors of the fingers. Involvement of the cervical sympathetic nerves indicates an injury at or above the ganglia and carries a much poorer prognosis for recovery. This can also occur with time in more distal lesions or incomplete palsy.

40   A B C E

The cervical lymph nodes are a common site for spread, with the node group involved depending on which part of the larynx is involved. The upper deep cervical nodes are involved in 40% of cases of carcinoma of the larynx. Types of tumour other than squamous cell carcinoma are very rare and include adenocarcinoma and basal cell carcinoma. Glottic tumours which present relatively early with persistent hoarseness are the commonest type of tumour (70%). The sex ratio is 10:1, Male:Female.

41   A D E

Ganglia are usually brilliantly translucent if accessible to a light source. They arise from myxoid degeneration of the tendon sheath or joint capsule, and not the nerve sheath. They often require no treatment. Multiple puncture and/or aspiration are recognized treatment strategies, but may not be successful. Melon seed bodies occur in tuberculous tenosynovitis.

42   A B C E

A persistent fever (PUO) is a rare but well recognized presentation of renal carcinoma and usually occurs in association with a raised ESR and anaemia. Poly(erythro)cythaemia due to ectopic erythropoetin is similarly rare (3%) but interesting! Renal tumours often spread as a tongue into the renal vein and may embolise (tumour emboli) especially during handling intraoperatively when massive pulmonary embolism may be fatal. Whilst a left varicocoele may occur with involvement of the left renal vein, hydrocoele has no association with renal tumours. Bony metastases which are usually osteolytic are well recognized.

43   C

Entamoeba histolytica is a protozoal parasite which affects up to 10% of the world's population. The trophozoites often inhabit the colon where they exist without symptoms living on faecal bacteria. In chronic carriers, more resistant cystic forms occur and they are passed into the stool from where they may be transmitted by the faeco–oral route. In active infection the trophozoites burrow through the mucosa and produce dysentery or an ulcerating colitis (with flask shaped ulcers) which may resemble inflammatory bowel disease and which can produce toxic dilatation. It is essential to consider the diagnosis in patients who have recently travelled to endemic areas, as steroids may exacerbate amoebic colitis and metronidazole may be curative. Amoebic liver abscess which results from seeding via the portal vein develops in <10% of cases of amoebic dysentery. The abscess is usually solitary and in 90% of cases involves the right lobe (posterolateral portion). It usually contains sterile pus (anchovy paste) which is best treated by percutaneous aspiration (it is important not to leave a drain *in situ* as this may lead to secondary infection). Only 20% of patients give a history of amoebic dysentery and only 12% have intestinal or hepatic trophozoites. These factors contribute to delay in diagnosis.

44 B C D

Percutaneous biopsy has classically been contraindicated to prevent contamination of tissue planes. Testicular tumours drain to pelvic lymph nodes whereas the scrotal skin drains to the inguinal lymph nodes. Most testicular tumours arise from germ cells and seminoma, in which the cells closely resemble spermatocytes, is common. Teratomas arise in the testis where pluripotential cells may contain ecto-, endo-, and mesodermal elements. Testicular tumour should be excluded in any (nonpubertal) man who presents with gynaecomastia. Tumour markers, including beta-HCG, (human chorionic gonadotrophin), pregnancy test and AFP, (alpha-fetoprotein) aid in the differential diagnosis and surveillance of testicular tumours during treatment.

45 B D

The sex incidence is similar although the age incidence is different reflecting the greater prevalence of alcoholic pancreatitis in young men. Renal and respiratory failure are common causes of death, which is usually the result of multisystem organ failure and which occurs in up to 15% of patients with severe pancreatitis. Between 3–30% of patients become hypocalcaemic. This is a poor prognostic feature and is thought to be due to increased glucagon and calcitonin levels and a deficiency in parathormone rather than increased binding of calcium in areas of fat necrosis. Pseudocyst and abscess formation often occur within the first two weeks. Treatment is usually conservative although delayed debridement may be required if aspiration and drainage fail to resolve a collection.

46 B D

The metaphysis is almost always (usually) affected first and the common-est organism is *Staphylococcus aureus*. Patients with sickle cell anaemia may be infected with *Salmonella* sp. If antibiotics are given early (within the first 48 hours) then surgical treatment is not usually required. The diagnosis is initially clinical. Radiological changes may not occur for 10 days. As infection spreads in the Haversian canals it causes thrombosis and bone infarction.

47 A C

The Barlow and von Rosen tests performed prior to discharge of all neonates are effective at detecting babies at risk of congenital dislocation. This condition which affects more girls than boys (between 3–5:1; F:M) is associated with breech position in late pregnancy and breech delivery. Only later if the femoral head comes out of the socket will the skin creases become noticeably abnormal. Very few children are walking at 5 months!!

48 C D

Colles' fracture is a fracture of the distal end of the radius produced by a fall on the outstretched hand and is said to have the characteristic 'dinner fork deformity'. The distal fragment is impacted, laterally angulated, dorsally angulated and displaced, and supinated. Treatment aims to correct these deformities! The old adage that 'if you have half a mind to be an orthopaedic surgeon, you have half a mind too much' just can't be true!!

49 C E

Vulval irritation is the presenting complaint in up to 10% of gynaecologi-cal out-patient attendances. It is not associated with carcinoma of the uterine body, but is a common symptom of vulval intra-epithelial neopla-sia and squamous cell carcinomas. The classic sign of trichomonal vaginitis is a frothy discharge that causes the symptom of intense vulval irritation and introital soreness. Cervical erosions or more correctly 'ectropion', are very common in postmenarchial and premenopausal women, they produce a clear non-irritant discharge. Excessive clothing may cause increased heat, moisture and friction in the area which predispose to fungal infections of the vulva, e.g. candida and tinea cruris, and may exacerbate pre-existing conditions.

50 A C E

Prolonged severe postpartum collapse from haemorrhage may be fol-lowed by ischaemic necrosis of the anterior lobe of the pituitary gland. If the patient survives, she will show features of Sheehan's syndrome (also called Simmonds' disease) where all the endocrine functions of the anterior pituitary are disturbed. Lack of thyrotrophic hormone results in lethargy, weight gain, cold intolerance and coarse dry skin. Lack of gonadotrophic hormones leads to genital and breast atrophy, amenorrhoea and loss of libido.

51 B C E

The major risk factors in cervical carcinoma are related to sexual activity. The condition is virtually unknown among celibate women. Early onset of sexual activity and promiscuity are the most significant risk factors in cervical carcinogenesis. Multiparity is indirectly associated with these factors, and therefore with the condition. Similarly, although prolonged oral contraception has an indirect positive association with cervical cancer, it cannot at present be interpreted as having a causal role. Male circumcision practised by orthodox Jews reduces the risk of exposure to smegma, implicated as a male aetiological factor in cervical cancer. The more likely explanation for the low incidence of cervical cancer in these women is their ethnically determined monogamous life-style.

52 B C D

The treatment of endometriosis can be medical, surgical or a combination of both approaches. If the disease is not extensive, diathermy cauterisation of the lesions at initial laparoscopic diagnosis may be adequate treatment. Progestogens may be given in large doses over 9 months to produce a 'pseudopregnancy' state and suppress menstruation. Between 70–95% of patients respond quickly to danazol which suppresses the hypothalamo-pituitary-ovarian axis and produces a 'pseudomenopause' state with consequent atrophy of ectopic endometrium. Surgical oophorectomy is the most effective available treatment to date. This is combined with hysterectomy and resection of lesions when other forms of treatment have failed.

53 A B C D E

Ethinyloestradiol is the most commonly used oestrogen in the combined contraceptive pill and is very potent in small doses given orally. Its side-effects include nausea and vomiting, weight gain or a bloated feeling due to water and sodium retention. Occasionally jaundice may result from hepatic cholestasis or obstruction from increased gall stone formation. Ethinyloestradiol elevates mood, depression caused by the combined pill is related to the progestogen component. Oestrogen therapy used unopposed without progesterones can cause overstimulation of the endometrium resulting in endometrial carcinoma in pre- and post-menopausal women.

54 B C
Diaphragms (sometimes referred to as Dutch caps) can be fitted by non-medically qualified personnel, who are specially trained in family planning techniques. It is important that the correct size is used to ensure a good fit. Some diaphragms are fitted with coiled springs. There is no need to resize diaphragms once they have been fitted unless the patient significantly changes weight/shape, e.g. after pregnancy.

55 A B C D
External cephalic version is the manoeuvre by which the foetus is turned from breech to cephalic presentation by manipulation through the mother's abdominal wall. It is not attempted before the 32nd week because in a large proportion of cases spontaneous cephalic version occurs by, and after, this time.   It is contraindicated in cases of pelvic contraction, antepartum haemorrhage, uterine scars, oligohydramnios, multiple pregnancy and intrauterine growth retardation (IUGR). The recognized risks of external version include foetal bradycardia due to placental separation or cord entanglement, premature rupture of membranes and precipitation of premature labour.

56 A B C D E
Extraction of impacted shoulders during vaginal breech delivery is facilitated by fracturing the clavicle. It requires no treatment and may well heal well without any deformity. The humerus may be fractured during difficulties with the arms in breech delivery. Excessive groin traction in difficult breech extraction can cause fractures of the femur which are usually greenstick and heal easily.   Healing of bony fractures is nearly always rapid and not associated with any deformity subsequently. Soft tissue bruising in neonates may occasionally be extensive enough to produce pathological jaundice and if the infant is thought to be at risk of developing kernicterus, an exchange transfusion may be required to lower the level of bilirubin.

57 A B D E
Pelvic sepsis, a recognized early complication of molar pregnancies, is no longer a serious problem with the wide range of antibiotics available. Secondary infection may occur due to instrumentation of the uterus or following colonisation of incomplete abortions by vaginal organisms.

Disseminated intravascular coagulation can develop when there is embolisation of trophoblastic tissue from the hydatidiform mole to the lungs. There is a 2–4% risk of choriocarcinoma developing after a hydatidiform mole. Early recognition of this condition is ensured by close surveillance of serum human chorionic gonadotrophin levels after evacuation of the uterus.

58 B C E
Varicose veins without evidence of deep vein thrombosis or during sclerosing therapy are not a contraindication to using the oral contraceptive pill. The increased mortality noted in women taking the pill compared to those who do not use it, is largely due to a fatal thromboembolic event, i.e. pulmonary embolism or cerebral or coronary thrombosis. Cholestasis of pregnancy, a common cause of pruritus in pregnancy, is a hormone-dependent phenomenon which is reproducible with oral contraceptive use. Similarly, carcinoma of the breast is hormone-sensitive and therefore an absolute contraindication to pill use. The combined contraceptive pill is an effective treatment for menorrhagia in women below the age of 35.

59 A C E
Proteinuria in pregnancy is usually identified by dipstick testing of the urine. Common causes of proteinuria in pregnancy include renal tract infections (e.g. acute pyelonephritis), renal disease (e.g. chronic glomerulonephritis and diabetic nephropathy), and pre-eclampsia. Significant proteinuria in pregnancy is defined as more than 500 mg/l of protein in a 24-hr collection of urine. Uncomplicated essential hypertension and abruptio placenta without pre-eclampsia are not associated with proteinuria.

60 A B C D E
Polyhydramnios often occurs with anencephaly and is thought to result partly from increased exudation from the exposed brain tissue and partly from the fact that the affected foetus does not swallow normally. Gestation is often prolonged in anencephalic pregnancies as the pituitary–adrenal axis crucial for the precise timing of parturition is poorly developed due to the presence of foetal adrenal hypoplasia. Anencephalic foetuses are more commonly female and may develop to a large size, producing shoulder dystocia at delivery.

ANSWERS TO PRACTICE EXAM 3

1   B D
Polyarteritis nodosa and most other forms of primary vasculitis are commoner in males. Polymyalgia rheumatica, however, is commoner in females. Ankylosing spondylitis and Reiter's syndrome are commoner in males. The male:female ratio in ankylosing spondylitis is probably in the region of 5:1(rather than 9:1 stated in most textbooks!). Females with atrial septal defect out-number males by 2:1. Patent ductus arteriosus is also more frequently found in females.

2   A E
There is accelerated 25-hydroxylation of 1-hydroxycholecalciferol in sarcoid lymph nodes leading to a vitamin D-mediated hypercalcaemia. The common endocrine cause of hypercalcaemia is hyperparathyroidism, but rarely, adrenal failure and hyperthyroidism can cause it. The serum calcium is usually normal in osteoporosis and Paget's disease, but slight elevation may be seen with either prolonged immobilization or multiple fractures. The calcium is low or normal in secondary hyperparathyroidism.

3   B E
Lithium toxicity causes cerebellar dysfunction, with a coarse tremor, ataxia and nystagmus. Long term treatment can cause renal failure and nephrogenic diabetes insipidus.

4   A C D E
Although there is some evidence that rheumatoid arthritis may have an infective trigger, no association with blood transfusion has been demonstrated. Retroviruses such as HIV and HTLV I are transmissable in blood, as are other viruses including Hepatitis B and C, Epstein-Barr and cytomegalovirus. Malarial parasites and treponemal parasites can also be transmitted by blood transfusion.

5   A E
Haemochromatosis is a condition in which there is widespread iron deposition: in the liver, heart and endocrine organs predominantly. Skin pigmentation is caused by an excess of melanin. Hepatocellular carcinoma can develop in the cirrhotic liver. Chondrocalcinosis and pseudogout may occur. Treatment is with desferrioxamine infusion.

6   C E

Hodgkin's disease is a malignancy that carries a good prognosis with treatment: 80% of cases will remit. Prognosis and therapy depend on stage and grade. Radiotherapy is used alone in localized disease. Bone marrow examination is used for staging purposes.

7   C

A wide pulse pressure (the difference between the systolic and diastolic pressures) is seen when there is a low peripheral vascular resistance, due either to vasodilatation or to 'run-off' states such as aortic regurgitation and persistent ductus arteriosus. Signs include a collapsing brachial pulse, visible carotid pulsation in the neck, capillary pulsation in the finger nails, and 'pistol shot' sounds heard over the femoral artery.

8   B D E

Acute closed angle glaucoma is the result of obstruction of the channels that drain the acqueous humour from the anterior chamber of the eye. It is often seen in those with a shallow anterior chamber and is precipitated by mydratics. Treatment is with miotics such as pilocarpine, and acetazolamide, a carbonic anhydrase inhibitor. Anterior chamber decompression can be best achieved surgically by iridotomy. Topical and systemic corticosteroids predispose to chronic simple glaucoma and cataracts.

9   A B C D

Bronchospasm is an allergic reaction to aspirin. It is also often associated with eczema. Salicylate poisoning produces tinnitus, deafness, vomiting and altered consciousness. Aspirin inhibits platelet aggregation but does not cause thrombocytopenia.

10   D

Phenytoin, trimethoprim-containing antibiotics and extensive psoriasis all cause folate deficiency; as do malabsorption, pregnancy and haemolytic anaemia. Vitamin B12 deficiency is caused by pernicious anaemia, gastrectomy, terminal ileal disease and small bowel bacterial overgrowth, which can occur in blind loops, diverticulae, and in the adynamic small bowel of scleroderma. Other gut manifestations of this disease include microstomia, oesophageal dysmotility and wide-based colonic diverticulae.

11   C D E

Convulsions with a temporal lobe focus are known as complex partial seizures because there is loss of consciousness without generalised tonic-clonic activity. There may be a characteristic aura of 'butterflies in the stomach' followed by olfactory, auditory or visual hallucinations. Then there is loss of consciousness during which there are stereotyped automative behaviours such as lip-smacking, sucking or chewing. Localized muscle twitching or numbness suggests discrete lesions in the motor or sensory cortex.

12 A B D E
The testes are atrophied in Klinefelter's syndrome and myotonic dystrophy. Cystic fibrosis patients have obstructive aspermia and those with haemochromatosis have hypogonadotrophic hypogonadism.

13 B C D E
Tuberculosis is usually caused by *Mycobacterium tuberculosis*. Lungs are the portal of entry via droplet inhalation. The primary infection is usually restricted to the lung but if haematogenous spread occurs there is multiple organ involvement (miliary tuberculosis). Primary infection is usually asymptomatic but post-primary TB, caused by reactivation of dormant tubercles characteristically produces a cavitating upper lobe pneumonia. Over the next five years the infection can spread to involve other organs including the renal tract and meninges. 4% of organisms in the UK are resistant to isoniazid (INH) in the laboratory. The majority of these will respond to a standard triple or quadruple therapeutic regime including isoniazid.

14 C D E
Malabsorption is caused by disruption of the luminal phase of digestion or its mucosal phase. Coeliac disease and giardiasis both impair this function of the small bowel mucosa. In jejunal diverticulosis, there is overgrowth of bacteria within the diverticulae resulting in interference with the function of bile acids and consequent malabsorption. Meckel's diverticulum is a cause of gastro-intestinal bleeding but not malabsorption.

15 A B D E
Phenobarbitone is a CNS depressant that causes paradoxical stimulation. Excitation is a rare consequence of anti-histamine treatment.

16 B D
Neuropathic (Charcot) joints undergo damage because the loss of position sensation in the surrounding tendons makes them vulnerable to injury.

Syringomyelia when severe causes dorsal column loss and the shoulder joints are particularly affected. Tabes dorsalis causes dorsal column loss but other forms of tertiary neurosyphilis do not. Diabetes mellitus causes a peripheral sensory neuropathy. There is no neuropathy associated with achondroplasia or septic arthritis.

17 C D E

Acute schizophrenia is a psychosis that can present with persecutory or grandiose delusions, auditory hallucinations in the form of remarks about the patient spoken in the third person or even a running commentary on his or her actions. There is a profound thought disorder in which the patient perceives their own thoughts as being taken away and the thoughts of others inserted in their place, and their actions as being controlled by an external force. Classically there is dual rather than multiple personality.

18 B D

The jugular venous pulse is abnormal in constrictive pericarditis. It is raised and the wave form has abrupt x and y descents. The pressure may rise paradoxically on inspiration as seen in acute tamponade (Kussmaul's sign) and a paradoxical pulse may be found in a third of patients. Auscultation may reveal a pericardial 'knock' (an early third sound). Signs of right heart failure with hepatic congestion, splenomegaly and ascites are characteristic. Pericardial calcification may be visible on plain X-ray even in asymptomatic patients. Pericardial friction rubs are rarely found with *constrictive* pericarditis.

19 B

Huntington's chorea and neurofibromatosis are autosomal dominant conditions. Haemophilia is X-linked recessive and haemochromatosis is thought to be polygenic.

20 A B E

A third heart sound is a low-pitched diastolic sound best heard at the left sternal edge in expiration. It can be a normal finding in children but usually represents abnormal filling of a dilated left ventricle with impaired systolic function. Left ventricular failure is commonly caused by ischaemic heart disease and systemic hypertension, aortic valve disease and mitral regurgitation. A third sound is commonly present in patients with significant mitral and aortic regurgitation due to early dilatation of the left ventricle. In aortic stenosis, left ventricular hypertrophy occurs with dilatation being present only in late or severe disease. A third heart sound may be present in constrictive pericarditis (pericardial knock) but is not a feature of uncomplicated pericarditis.

21 **A D**

The signs of a facial nerve palsy will depend on the site of the lesion. Disease proximal to the nerve's entry into the petrous temporal bone will cause decreased lacrimation. A lesion within the petrous temporal causes hyperacusis as the nerve to stapedius is involved. The chordae tympani provide taste sensation to the anterior two-thirds of the tongue and separate from the main nerve as it exits from the facial canal in the middle ear. Although the eyelid is unaffected (third nerve), there is impairment of eye closure. Patients with upper motor neurone lesions of the facial nerve may be able to wrinkle the forehead of the affected side because of bilateral cortical innervation. Motor innervation of the tongue (twelfth nerve) and corneal sensation (fifth nerve) will be unaffected.

22 **C D**

The common causes of atrial fibrillation are ischaemic and hypertensive heart disease, followed by rheumatic mitral valve disease, thyrotoxicosis and heart muscle disorders including alcoholic and idiopathic cardiomyopathies. If atrial fibrillation is present in a patient with aortic stenosis, one should suspect the possibility of coexisting mitral valve disease. Dressler's syndrome is an immune-mediated pericarditis occuring characteristically four to six weeks after myocardial infarction.

23 **A B**

Hyponatraemia is commonly a result of hypovolaemia, which is a stimulus to the secretion of anti-diuretic hormone. Hypotension may be present. Overuse of diuretics is a common cause, particularly in the elderly. It is frequently compounded by rehydration with intravenous dextrose solutions. Treatment of cases by normalising vascular filling pressure with colloid and then fluid restricting are usually successful. Rarely hypertonic saline will have to be given. Attention must be paid to supportive measures as patients can have a reduced level of consciousness and grand mal fits. In Conn's syndrome, the serum sodium is either raised or normal. Tetany may occur in the presence of hyperkalaemia.

24 **C D**

Papilloedema is a swelling of the optic disc caused by a rise in cerebrospinal fluid pressure. Early signs include loss of spontaneous venous pulsation and hyperaemia. As the disc swells the nasal margin is the first to become indistinct. In severe cases flame-shaped haemorrhages will appear. Swelling of the disc can also be caused by inflammation or ischaemia of the nerve head and systemic hypertension. Visual acuity is little affected until late in the condition when visual loss is of peripheral vision and enlargement of blind spots. Disc pallor is a feature of optic atrophy or neuritis.

25 A B D E
The most common cause of iron deficiency worldwide is hookworm infestation (*Ancylostoma duodenale* and *Necator americanus*). Away from the gastrointestinal tract, menorrhagia and pregnancy are common causes, which explains the increased prevalence in women of child-bearing age. Serum iron and ferritin levels are low. Total iron binding capacity may be raised.

26 A B C D
Gout is often an acute monoarthritis or additive oligoarthritis caused by an inflammatory response to urate crystals precipitating in the joints. It can subside without joint damage or cause characteristic punched out peri-articular bone erosions. In the chronic form, the crystals can form deposits around joints, bursae or under the skin (tophi) or result in an obstructive uropathy due to the formation of renal stones. Uric acid is the end product of purine metabolism.

27 B D E
Bone resorption in multiple myeloma is a non-osteoclast-mediated process and therefore hypercalcaemia develops in the absence of a rise in alkaline phosphatase.

28 A D
Skin involvement in sarcoidosis is not macular. Erythema nodosum occurs in acute sarcoidosis. Lupus pernio and discrete maculopapular lesions are seen in the chronic form of the disease. Mumps causes localised cervical lymphadenopathy and usually no rash. The rash in chickenpox is vesicular.

29 C D E
The superior vena cava returns blood from the head, upper limbs and upper part of the trunk. The pulmonary valve regulates blood leaving the right ventricle of the heart.

30 C D E

Bacteroides are obligate anaerobes. They are Gram-negative rods of varying morphology and are classed as 'coccobacilli'. They are sensitive to aminoglycosides and to metronidazole.

31 B E

Bile stained vomiting is always a worrying sign implying intestinal obstruction. Meconium may be distal to the obstruction and passed after birth, hence its passage does not exclude an obstruction. X-rays may be useful for example showing the double bubble of duodenal atresia or free air seen in perforation of the bowel or air within the bowel wall as in necrotising enterocolitis. Hirschsprung's disease is five times commmoner in males than females.

32 D E

A child starts to transfer from hand to hand from 28 weeks or more. A voluntary smile comes by about 6 weeks and hearing assessments are usually performed at about 6 to 8 months of age.

33 B C D E

The use of star charts and a reward system is primarily encouraged. The urine should always be examined for the presence of a urinary tract infection and the child examined to exclude the presence of a neurological disorder.

34 C

Subcapital (intracapsular) fractures of the femur may cause avascular necrosis of the head of the femur. Scaphoid fractures which interrupt the blood supply which enters entirely through the distal pole have a propensity to necrosis. Other sites include the navicular, talus and lunate. Supracondylar humeral (not shaft) fractures can produce a Volkmann's ischaemia of the forearm due to brachial artery injury.

35 A C D

Hallux valgus both before and after treatment is associated with hammer toes where the 2nd, 3rd and 4th toes become hyperextended at the metatarsophalangeal and distal interphalangeal (d.i.p.) joints causing callosities over the bony prominence of the proximal interphalangeal joint. The 'striking' toe pad distinguishes hammer toes from claw toes where the d.i.p. joint is flexed.

36   A D E

A closed fracture of the femur leads to at least a litre of blood loss. Sciatic nerve damage is rare. Fat embolism which may follow any long bone fracture, is commonest in femoral fracture. Fracture distal to a prosthesis is a well recognised and serious complication of joint replacement. Haemarthrosis follows a joint injury.

37   A C E

A lignocaine–adrenaline mixture is often utilised for the reduction in arteriolar bleeding as it causes contraction of vascular smooth muscle. This is why it is specifically contraindicated in sites or organs with end arteries such as the digits, the nose, the ear and the penis. A hypertensive crisis may be precipitated in patients on MAOIs. Although caution should be exercised there is no specific contraindication in patients with cardiac disease.

38   A D

Rest pain is a symptom of critical ischaemia and frequently precedes or is associated with ulceration and gangrene. It is usually worse at night when cardiac output falls. This is why arteriopaths sit out in a chair or hang their leg over the edge of the bed in order to increase blood flow by gravity. Elevation will not usually be tolerated. It most commonly affects the forefoot and even with continuous opiate infusion may be intractable.

39   B C D

A tourniquet may increase stasis and produce local injury. Early mobilization is thought to be important and graduated calf compression and intraoperative calf compression have been shown to reduce the incidence of deep vein thrombosis. The oral contraceptive pill (the only hormone taken by large numbers of patients undergoing surgery) may increase the risk of deep vein thrombosis.

40   A D E

After a full history and examination, which may suggest the presence of a benign macrocyst, mammography and fine needle aspiration (FNA) cytology are usually performed for all palpable masses. If the mass is a diffuse thickening which fluctuates with the cycle and is painful, then it is likely to be benign breast disease (mastalgia/fibroadenosis). Enlarged lymph nodes are not specific for cancer and up to 30% of palpable nodes in patients with cancer are benign. A fibroadenoma is usually a charac-teristic firm painless mobile mass, and in a younger woman, once the diagnosis has been established (mammography/ultrasound scan/FNA) may be simply observed, as some resolve spontaneously.

41 B D E

It is usually due to a nodular thickening of the palmar fascia and affects the ring and little fingers most commonly. It more rarely affects the sole (plantar fascia) and the penis (Peyronie's). It occurs rarely in women. In its early stages it can be managed by splinting and physiotherapy.

42 A D E

If the membranous urethra is injured or if the external sphincter is damaged incontinence can occur. Retrograde ejaculation is common due to incontinence of the bladder neck. Urethral not ureteric stricture may occur. Carcinoma of the prostate is an incidental finding in many patients having transurethral resection of the prostate (TURP). The incidence of cancer is not subsequently increased.

43 A B D

Most cancers (75%) of the tongue occur on the (anterior) oral portion, most often on the lateral border of the middle third. Smoking (and all the other S's!!; syphilis, sepsis, sharp teeth, spirits, spices and candidiasis) predisposes to cancer in the oral cavity. The overall prognosis (<50% cure) is worse than in carcinoma of the lip (>70%); although small peripheral lesions can be cured (75–80% 5 year survival) by excision and larger lesions without spread to regional lymph nodes or the floor of the mouth can be successfully (40–55%) treated without loss of function by radioactive implants. The sex incidence is now similar due to the changing smoking habits of men (women continue to smoke).

44 A C D

Haemorrhage which characteristically presents as an episode of profuse bright red rectal bleeding not precipitated by defaecation is a well recognised complication of diverticular disease. Colonic cancer must be considered in the differential diagnosis but is not associated with the presence of diverticular disease. Fistula formation with the skin and adjacent organs including the bladder (causing pneumaturia – air in the urine) is a complication of inflammation of a diverticulum causing perforation and abscess formation with subsequent fistula formation. Pseudopolyps are a feature of ulcerative colitis and are descriptive of the areas of inflamed oedematous and swollen mucosa adjacent to ulcerated areas of colon.

45 B C E

Loss of sensation over the anatomical snuff box is caused by an injury to the radial nerve (superficial cutaneous branch). Injury to the median nerve (C678,T1) is commonly at the wrist after it has supplied the following muscles: pronator teres, flexor carpi radialis, palmaris longus, flexor digitorum profundus, and pronator quadratus. In the hand it usually supplies the radial two lumbricals, opponens pollicis, abductor pollicis brevis, and the outer head of flexor pollicis brevis (remember 'LOAF'). It sometimes supplies the first dorsal interosseous (the rest being supplied by the ulnar nerve). Sensory loss depends on the level of division but includes the palmar aspect of the thumb, index and middle finger, and radial aspect of the ring finger. A variable part of the dorsum of these fingers is also supplied by the median nerve.

46 A C D

Fistula *in ano* is a condition where there is an abnormal tract, lined by granulation tissue, from the lining of the anus or rectum, leading to the perianal skin. Leukaemic patients have a greatly increased incidence of anorectal disorders, particularly fissure *in ano* but including fistula *in ano*. In all patients with a fistula, a biopsy should be performed to exclude Crohn's disease and more rarely anorectal malignancy. Neither diverticular disease nor ischaemic colitis are associated with fistula *in ano*.

47 A C E

Multinodular goitre (demonstrated on thyroid scanning) may present with a solitary palpable nodule (or a dominant nodule in a clinically nodular goitre). In both situations the possibility that the nodule is neoplastic should be considered. 10% of clinically solitary nodules are malignant. Although scanning and fine needle aspiration cytology have enabled some groups to advocate selective surgery, the standard advice is to recommend thyroid lobectomy for a solitary nodule. Thyroid neoplasms (benign and malignant) are more common in women. Because of the proximity of the oesophagus any goitre may cause dysphagia.

48 A C

Crohn's disease which commonly affects the terminal ileum and may therefore cause altered enterohepatic circulation of bile is associated with an increased incidence of gallstones. Spherocytosis and other haemolytic anaemias will cause an increase in bile pigments leading to pigment stone formation. Pernicious anaemia, renal stones and cirrhosis are not associated with gallstones.

49 C D

Human colostrum is a yellow fluid secreted in small amounts from the breasts after about 12 weeks' gestation. For the first two days after childbirth an increased amount of colostrum is secreted by the breast acini. It is rich in fat globules, minerals and the antibodies IgA and IgG. It has moderate amounts of protein and small amounts of carbohydrates. Because of its high fat content it is very calorific. Colostrum IgA helps combat infectious agents and other antigens.

50 A C E

Approximately 25% of placental abruptions are associated with proteinuria and hypertension. It is not clear whether proteinuric hypertension predisposes to abruption. Proteinuria may often follow rather than precede abruption. Painless vaginal bleeding is a feature of placenta praevia, whereas patients with placental abruption present with varying degrees of constant abdominal pain and shock which is often out of proportion to the amount of blood lost vaginally. The uterus is often tender and in severe abruptions may be woody hard due to tonic uterine contraction. Foetal parts are difficult to feel in such cases. Foetal malpresentation is associated with placenta praevia rather than placental abruption.

51 A B

Carcinoma of the body of the uterus is typically a disorder of postmenopausal women, but in 25% of cases it can occur before the menopause and in 5% of these, the women are aged less than 40. The classic symptom is irregular peri- or post-menopausal bleeding, but an early symptom in some women is a watery discharge. Pain denotes extensive spread of disease and is therefore a late symptom. Uterine enlargement is usually slight to moderate, and pelvic examination is often unremarkable. Occasionally the condition presents as a vaginal nodule, the diagnosis being reached on biopsy.

52 B D

Secondary or congestive dysmenorrhoea refers to painful periods for which an organic or psychosexual cause exists. It usually starts as a dull ache a few days before the menses and intensifies up to the time of menstruation. Antispasmodics and cervical dilatation may be helpful in primary or spasmodic dysmenorrhoea, but not in secondary dysmenorrhoea where treatment should be aimed at eliminating the underlying cause.

53 A B E

A hiatus hernia or oesophageal reflux can cause 'waterbrash' or regurgitation of acid stomach contents. This is made worse by pressure on the stomach from the enlarging uterus in late pregnancy. Vomiting and epigastric pain can occur in fulminating pre-eclampsia, indicating subhepatic haemorrhages or necrosis. Acute pyelonephritis usually presents with pyrexia, rigors and repeated vomiting in the second half of the pregnancy. Hydatidiform mole and hyperemesis gravidarum, on the other hand, may present with persistent vomiting in the first few weeks of pregnancy.

54 A B C D E

In 95% of ectopic pregnancies the site of implantation is the Fallopian tube. Ovarian ectopic pregnancies may be *primary*, when implantation occurs directly on the ovary, or *secondary*, when tubal abortion occurs with re-implantation on the ovary. Pelvic adhesions in endometriosis can cause tubal distortion and the fertilised egg may be trapped within the tube where it subsequently implants. Progesterone decreases tubal motility and delays ovum transport into the uterus. Tubal abortion is the most common outcome of tubal ectopic pregnancy, occurring within a few weeks of implantation.

55 B D E

Once cord prolapse is diagnosed and if the foetus is alive, the treatment is *immediate* delivery. If the cervix is fully dilated and the presentation is cephalic with no contraindications to instrumental delivery, immediate delivery with forceps should be performed. If the cervix is not fully dilated, immediate Caesarean section is indicated. While preparations are being made for delivery, the cord should be replaced inside the vagina and the presenting part digitally disimpacted off the cervix and held there till delivery of the foetus is achieved. If foetal demise is confirmed by ultrasound, and there are no contraindications to a vaginal delivery, labour is allowed to continue as normal.

56 A D E

Foetal malformations causing polyhydramnios include anencephaly, spina bifida, oesophageal and bowel atresia. Polyhydramnios is not caused by ascites or ovarian cysts in the mother or foetus although it is associated with foetal ascites. It is seen when maternal diabetes is poorly controlled. In the majority of cases the excess liquor accumulates slowly and is only noticed after the 30th week. Spontaneous preterm labour is common.

57 A B

Chronic pelvic inflammatory disease resembles pelvic endometriosis in its clinical presentation. Common symptoms are pelvic pain, deep dyspareunia, infertility and menorrhagia. Occasionally endometriosis involves the muscular wall of the bowel, causing dense fibrosis and intestinal obstruction. The presence of tender nodules on pelvic examination is very suggestive of endometriosis. Endometriosis of the bladder is very rare and when present causes frequency of micturition and haematuria, but bladder control is maintained.

58 A B C D

Premature infants account for 66% of low birth weight (<2.5kg) babies. Their weight may be appropriate for their gestational age, or they may be small-for-dates in addition to being premature. The preterm infant is more susceptible to birth trauma with the potential complications of cerebral palsy, intellectual impairment, visual and hearing deficits. Small babies have little subcutaneous fat insulation and a large surface area relative to their weight, which allows rapid heat loss. In addition, they lack the thermogenic brown adipose tissue seen in more mature babies. Hypoglycaemia may be due to a lack of glycogen stores in the liver and also because these infants are unable to swallow their feeds properly.

59 A B C D E

Antibodies from the mother cross the placenta and coat the foetal erythrocytes, leading to their destruction by the reticuloendothelial system. This haemolysis can result in profound foetal anaemia. In severe cases there is generalised oedema of the foetus (hydrops foetalis) with pleural, pericardial and peritoneal effusions. Foetal death often ensues. Severe pre-eclampsia may be seen in conjunction with foetal or placental hydrops for any reason including rhesus disease.

60 A B D

Uterine rupture in labour usually *results* from prolonged violent uterine contractions. Signs of uterine rupture include foetal distress or death, severe maternal shock with evidence of intra-abdominal and vaginal bleeding. Contractions usually cease once the foetus is extruded out of the uterus into the peritoneal cavity. Amniotic fluid embolism may result from the hypertonic uterine contractions leading up to uterine rupture, however embolisation is usually associated with small tears in the uterus, cervix and vagina rather than with complete disruption of the uterine wall as in rupture.

ANSWERS TO PRACTICE EXAM 4

1   A B C D E
Common causes of an exudative pleural effusion include malignant disease of the lung or pleura, pyogenic infection in the lung (parapneumonic effusion) or pleural space (empyema), and tuberculosis. Less common are Dressler's syndrome and the connective tissue disorders. Transudative effusions are caused by right heart failure and hypoproteinaemia. Uraemia and hypothyroidism are rarer causes of effusions and pulmonary infarction sometimes causes a small blood-stained effusion. Pleural involvement in sarcoidosis is very rarely seen, but can occur.

2   D E
Systemic lupus erythematosus is characteristically associated with a facial butterfly rash. Rosacea can mimic this appearance. Other causes of a butterfly rash include lupus pernio (sarcoidosis), lupus vulgaris (tuberculosis), erysipelas (*Streptococcus pyogenes* infection) and photosensitive dermatoses. A malar flush is seen in mitral stenosis. Pityriasis rosea occurs mainly on the trunk. Vitiligo and scleroderma can occur at any site.

3   B C E
A raised serum alkaline phosphatase can be seen in acute pancreatitis due to gall-stone impaction at the ampulla of Vater with consequent common bile duct obstruction. Early removal of the stone via endoscopic retrograde cholangiopancreatography improves the prognosis.

4   A C E
Von Willebrand's disease is a mild and usually autosomal dominant haemostatic disorder. There is a deficiency of von Willebrand factor, which causes platelet adhesion and prevents the breakdown of Factor VIII in the circulation. Diagnosis is suggested by finding a prolonged bleeding time and kaolin partial thromboplastin time (KPPT), and can be made using the ristocetin aggregation test. In severe haemorrhage cryoprecipitate and DDAVP (1-deamino-8-D-arginine vasopressin) are effective.

5   A C D
Biguanides lower blood glucose by enhancing its peripheral utilization in the presence of insulin and by inhibiting gluconeogenesis in the liver. They are used in the treatment of non-insulin dependent diabetes mellitus,

often in the obese or as an adjunct to sulphonylureas. Lactic acidosis is a complication and can be distinguished from ketoacidosis by normoglycaemia, the lack of ketonuria and elevation of serum lactate. Sulphonylureas should be used initially, and there is a tendency to prescribe biguanides only if other drugs have failed to achieve adequate control.

6   C

The headache of meningitis is associated with photophobia, neck stiffness and drowsiness. Patients tend to keep still as movement aggravates the headache. Patients are usually febrile. Kernig's sign (an inability to extend the knee fully with the hip flexed) may be positive.

7   A B

Digoxin is renally excreted and glomerular filtration rate falls with increasing age, thus rendering the elderly susceptible to digoxin toxicity. The drug is an inhibitor of the membrane sodium-potassium ATPase and is more toxic when plasma potassium is low.

8   A B C D E

Secondary causes of hypertension include endocrine causes (including Cushing's syndrome, Conn's syndome and phaeochromocytoma) and renal causes. Either intrinsic renal disease or renovascular disease can cause high blood pressure. Atherosclerosis can result in renal artery stenosis. Chronic alcoholism results in moderate increases in blood pressure due to vasoconstriction in the muscle beds.

9   A B C D E

In Hodgkin's disease with bone involvement, pain is often a feature with or without fracture. Sclerotic opacities may be seen on X-ray. Vertebral involvement with lymphomatous deposits can cause extradural cord compression and an acute paraplegia. A synovitis can occur due either to direct infiltration by lymphomatous tissue or as a reactive synovitis related to juxta-articular bony deposits.

10   A B C

Urinary incontinence is common in elderly females. It can be due to structural factors in the lower urinary tract (vaginal prolapse), urinary tract infection, drugs such as diuretics and any central nervous system disease, commonly dementia. Chlorpromazine causes urinary retention due to its antimuscarinic effect. Another antimuscarinic drug, oxybutinin, is used in the treatment of incontinence. Uncomplicated vaginitis does not in itself cause urinary incontinence, however symptoms of a urinary tract infection are commoner in patients with vaginitis.

11 B D
Monocular visual loss is due to disease in the visual pathway anterior to the optic chiasm. Causes include ptosis due to third nerve palsy, strabismus in childhood, scarring keratitis, acute angle-closure glaucoma, iridocyclitis, cataract, vitreous haemorrhage, retinal detachment and optic nerve disorders including optic neuritis and infarction (atheroma or giant cell arteritis). Occipital lobe tumours and subdural haematomata may result in disruption of the visual pathway posterior to the optic chiasm resulting in homonymous hemianopia. Lead poisoning results in encephalopathy and a predominantly motor neuropathy. Although optic atrophy may occur, signs and symptoms are usually bilateral.

12 A B D E
There is a long list of causes of convulsions. They can be divided into structural lesions affecting the brain (e.g. subdural haematoma), and systemic metabolic disorders that lower the seizure threshold (e.g. hyponatraemia). Down's syndrome leads to premature Alzheimer's disease, which causes seizures in advanced cases.

13 A
A narrow pulse pressure is caused by limitation of systolic arterial pressure by left ventricular outflow obstruction. A slow rising 'plateau' pulse with a narrow pulse pressure is characteristic of aortic stenosis.

14 C D E
Depression is a disorder of low mood. Diurnal variation is common with mood lowest on waking. Psychotic symptoms can occur with delusions and hallucinations, often accusatory in tone ('he is wicked'). Neurovegetative or biological symptoms include anorexia, constipation, loss of libido, and waking in the early hours of the morning.

15 A B C D E
Diseases of the adrenal glands leading to endocrine under-production include auto-immune destruction (Addison's disease), tuberculosis and haemorrhagic infarction in the context of meningococcaemia (Waterhouse–Friedrichson syndrome). Hypocorticalism also occurs in pituitary failure

or suppression of endogenous ACTH production by exogenous steroid administration.

16 A C

The S1 nerve root provides motor innervation to the hip and knee extensors and the ankle plantar-flexors. Its dermatome covers the lateral aspect of the foot, the heel and the back of the calf. It mediates the hamstring and ankle jerk; the latter is in more common use clinically. Disc herniation causes pain via dural tension, which is increased in the lower lumbar and sacral region by lifting the leg straight up with the patient supine (the 'sciatic' stretch test). Hyperextension of the hip with the knee flexed increases upper lumbar dural tension (the 'femoral' stretch test).

17 A C D

Intravenous iodine is actively taken up by the thyroid gland, and thus provides a mechanism for targetting the hyper-secreting gland with ionising radiation. It should be avoided in women of child-bearing age. Getting the dose right is difficult, and patients often end up being hypothyroid, requiring thyroxine replacement therapy. There is a small increased risk of subsequent thyroid cancer.

18 A B C D

Causes of generalized lymphadenopathy can be divided into infections, lymphoreticuloses, and inflammatory disorders. The latter group is the smallest and includes Still's disease, rheumatoid arthritis and sarcoidosis. Cat scratch disease causes localised lymphadenopathy.

19 A C D E

Cheyne-Stokes respiration is the name given to a pattern of breathing in which series of large tidal volume gasps are punctuated by periods of apnoea. The pattern of breathing is characteristic in that there is a crescendo pattern, building up gradually to the large gasps followed by the period of apnoea. It is caused by dysfunction of the brain stem respiratory centre and heralds death. Cheyne-Stokes respiration can therefore be seen in association with a number of different predisposing conditions. Patients with obstructive airway disease are capable of small tidal volumes only.

20 E

Somatic signs of anxiety are mainly caused by sympathetic autonomic over-activity. They therefore include tachycardia, sweating, tremor and urgency of bowel motion. Back pain and headache can result from muscle tension. Dry mouth is more likely than drooling.

21 A B C D E
The herpes virus group comprises herpes simplex, Epstein-Barr, cytomegalovirus and varicella zoster, which is responsible for chickenpox. Hyperimmune globulin administered within 72 hours of contact is preventative, otherwise the condition responds to treatment with acyclovir. This is only indicated in those with meningoencephalitis and the immunosuppressed. The incubation period is 14–21 days, however the prodromal phase of the illness is only 1–2 days or less.

22 A C D E
Gynaecomastia may occur and galactorrhoea as a result of ectopic hormone production of prolactin. A myasthenic syndrome can occur as a non-metastatic manifestation of bronchial carcinoma. Painful wrists and ankles are due to hypertrophic pulmonary osteoarthropathy (HPOA) which is associated with finger clubbing. Hypokalaemia may be found in tumours secreting adrenocorticotrophic hormone (ACTH) and hyponatraemia is common due to inappropriate anti-diuretic hormone (ADH) secretion.

23 A B D E
Pleural effusions and pneumothoraces may displace the mediastinum and trachea towards the opposite side. Collapse of the lung will 'pull' the mediastinal structures towards the side of the lesion. Mediastinal masses such as enlarged nodes, goitre, thymus gland or developmental cysts can displace the trachea to either side. A large pericardial effusion may result in splaying of the carina but will not displace the trachea laterally.

24 B C E
Hypercalcaemia may be a cause of depression and renal failure. There is an increased incidence of peptic ulceration in patients with primary hyperparathyroidism. Primary hyperparathyroidism also causes bone pain, urolithiasis, keratopathy and can precipitate acute pancreatitis.

25 A D
In Hodgkin's disease, lymphocyte-depleted histology carries the worst prognosis. Prognosis however with nodular sclerosing and lymphocyte predominant histology or in early disease may be good. Stage 1 disease is usually treated with localized radiotherapy. Chemotherapy may be used

if there are 'B' symptoms. Splenectomy used to be performed for staging purposes and does not improve prognosis. Bone marrow examination is not necessary to make the diagnosis; lymph node biopsy can achieve this, but both may be helpful in staging.

26 A B C D

Characteristic features of myocardial infarction include chest pain with radiation to the left arm or neck. A low grade fever may be present. Pericarditis may occur with full thickness infarcts in the acute phase. In addition, pleuropericarditis can be a complication 2–6 weeks after the event (Dressler's syndrome). A more common complication, early or late, is left ventricular failure, which can cause blood-stained frothy sputum.

27 A C

Other skin conditions related to sunlight include reactions to certain drugs, systemic lupus erythematosus and the cutaneous porphyrias. Chloasma is most commonly induced by pregnancy or by taking the oral contraceptive pill, but the hyperpigmentation may be exacerbated by sunlight.

28 E

In mitral stenosis with a pliable valve there might be an opening snap and the first heart sound is usually accentuated. The apex beat is usually described as 'tapping'. Atrial fibrillation may be seen in both conditions. A third heart sound indicates rapid ventricular filling and therefore does not occur in mitral stenosis.

29 B D

Clorpromazine-induced jaundice is rare. It occurs one to three weeks after the instigation of therapy and can be associated with fever and peripheral blood eosinophilia. Liver histology shows obstruction of canaliculi with bile thrombi. Methyltestosterone causes cholestasis without structural liver damage.

30 D E

Azathioprine is now in widespread use for the treatment of connective tissue and other inflammatory diseases. It can be used as a steroid-sparing agent or as monotherapy. Azathioprine is metabolised by xanthine oxidase to its inactive form, and the dose must be reduced during treatment with the xanthine oxidase inhibitor, allopurinol.

31 A B C D

Metabolic disorders may give rise to hypoglycaemia and affect neurodevelopment, e.g. with galactosaemia and glycogen storage disease. Duchenne muscular dystrophy is an X-linked disease associated with development delay and cardiomyopathy. Marfan's syndrome is associated with a normal neurodevelopmental outcome.

32 C D

Oestrogens are given to teenage girls to encourage the development of secondary sexual characteristics as the ovarian tissue is usually absent or poorly functioning; hence these girls also have primary amenorrhoea. Osteoporosis is a recognized feature with coarse trabeculation being common.

33 C E

Anatomical and physiological changes in the acidity of secretions tend to be the underlying cause of this condition. Sexual abuse may be a cause, as may threadworms.

34 A D

Fournier's gangrene may appear spontaneously or after minor surgery in previously fit patients. They develop a spreading superficial gangrene affecting the perineum and often exposing the entire scrotal contents. It is most often caused by a haemolytic microaerophilic streptococcus. Testicular gangrene may rarely ensue but is not the cause of the infection. Patients are usually systemically unwell, including a high fever.

35 A B C D

Multifocal ductal carcinoma *in situ* is being increasingly recognized as a result of breast screening. Mastectomy is often recommended because of its multifocal nature and the good prognosis when treated by mastectomy. The long thoracic nerve of Bell (C567) supplies the serratus anterior muscle and is at risk of injury, which presents as winging of the scapula, in patients undergoing mastectomy. The nerve to latissimus dorsi (C5678), which must be preserved as it may be required for reconstruction in a myocutaneous flap, is also at risk. Paget's disease also has a good prognosis when treated by mastectomy. The internal mammary artery is not routinely divided as part of a mastectomy. In supraradical mastectomy, which is an obsolete operation with no place in modern surgery, the internal mammary artery was divided during clearance of the internal mammary chain of lymph nodes.

36 B C D

There is no association between thyroid surgery and intracerebral infection. An intracerebral abscess causes considerable surrounding brain oedema and may cause a rapid rise in intracranial pressure. Lumbar puncture is therefore contraindicated. Attic perforation following middle ear infection is a classic cause of intracerebral abscess. Intracerebral abscess may very occasionally present with symptoms which are classic for meningitis (neck stiffness and photophobia).

37 B D

Sigmoid volvulus classically presents with a sudden onset of left iliac fossa pain and abdominal distension. It is most common in this country in institutionalised and elderly patients and patients may have had previous episodes of abdominal pain. They usually have chronic constipation. A history of altered bowel habit or recent constipation is more suggestive of an intraluminal obstruction. Examination of the abdomen reveals a tensely distended tympanitic abdomen and sigmoidoscopy (rigid or flexible) is both diagnostic and therapeutic, possibly combined with a flatus tube. In large bowel obstruction, regardless of its aetiology, vomiting is usually a late symptom.

38 A B E

Gastric cancer is more common in patients with blood group A. (One can remember this because it was first described by the distinguished gastro-enterologist, Aird). Both type 1 and type 11 chronic atrophic gastritis are associated with an increased incidence of gastric cancer. Gastric cancer is most common in the antrum and prepyloric regions. After gastric surgery iron deficiency occurs in up to 40% of patients due to decreased absorption of organic iron. Blood loss due to stomal ulcer or other malignancy must be excluded in these patients. Vitamin B12 deficiency causing anaemia is rare but between 15 and 30% of patients have reduced levels of B12. Keratoacanthoma is not premalignant but squamous cell carcinoma must be considered in the differential diagnosis.

39 D

Tetanus is caused by an anaerobic Gram-positive rod *Clostridium tetani* which produces a potent neurotoxin, that spreads proximally in motor nerves and via the blood stream. Affected muscles are hypertonic and violent, often painful spasms are triggered by trivial stimuli. The shorter the gap between the first symptom and the first reflex spasm the worse the prognosis. Active immunity can be produced by the administration of a course of adsorbed tetanus toxoid. Passive immunity in at risk patients can be produced by use of human antitetanus globulin. Tetany (carpopedal spasm) is due to hypocalcaemia (rarely hypomagnesaemia) and may be treated by intravenous calcium.

40 A C D

Dehiscence is rare (<2%) and usually occurs between the 6th and 8th days after surgery. It is commonly preceded by a serosanguineous discharge of peritoneal fluid. It may occur in uninfected wounds and is more common in upper midline wounds. It most commonly affects the elderly, malnourished patients or patients with malignancy.

41 A D E

Leucoplakia is a clinical descriptive term to describe white patches on the oral mucosa which cannot be ascribed to a particular disease. There is commonly keratinisation of the mucosa. Only 4% become malignant over a 20 year follow up. Spontaneous remission is rare although leucoplakia associated with dental problems may regress if the problem is treated. Malignancy is more common when leucoplakia is seen on the floor of the mouth, on the lateral margins of the tongue, and in the elderly.

42 A C E

Escharotomies (longitudinal relieving incisions) are indicated for circumferential burns,which may cause distal ischaemia and impaired venous return in limbs or digits and reduced chest expansion if occurring on the chest wall. Tracheostomy should be avoided by prompt intubation as it may be associated with overwhelming infection. Compression garments may reduce scarring during recovery. The greatest fluid losses occur in the first 12 hours. *Pseudomonas* is a common cause of infection in burns patients.

43 A B E

Up to 70% of patients with early breast cancer (most patients now present with early disease) can be 'cured' by appropriate management which may include tamoxifen in both premenopausal and postmenopausal women (and men, who generally have a poorer prognosis partly because they usually have more advanced tumours). Oophorectomy has a definite place (survival advantage) in the management of premenopausal women and is useful in women with metastatic (particularly bony) disease. Lymphoedema may follow both surgery and radiotherapy to the axilla, and may result from axillary node involvement. It is often difficult to manage.

44 A B C
Abdominal aortic aneurysm is associated with aneurysms at other sites including the femoral and popliteal arteries. There is a familial predisposition to aneurysm formation and first degree male relatives of patients with aneurysms have a high incidence on screening. Renal colic presenting in an elderly patient without a previous history of renal stones should be assumed to be due to a leaking aortic aneurysm until proved otherwise. Surgery involves an inlay technique not resection.

45 C D E
Most rib tumours are due to secondaries, usually from lung and breast cancer. These are usually painful and may cause pathological fractures. Multiple myeloma may affect the ribs. Benign tumours (e.g. chondroma) should be removed to establish a diagnosis and to prevent sarcomatous change.

46 A C
Anterior dislocation of the shoulder may damage the axillary nerve causing loss of sensation over deltoid. Posterior fracture dislocation of the hip may produce sciatic nerve injury in up to 10% of patients. This usually affects the lateral popliteal component of the nerve (foot drop). Fracture of the *humerus* produces *radial* nerve injury. Tibial shaft and clavicular fractures are rarely associated with nerve injury.

47 A B C
All arteriovenous fistulae have a structural and physiological effect. If large and persistent they will produce an increase in pulse pressure (systolic–diastolic), pulse rate and cardiac output. They may produce distal gangrene. Venous pressure increases. Limb *hypertrophy* is seen in congenital arteriovenous fistulae.

48 A B D
Pyloric stenosis (where the patient vomits gastric acid) will produce a partially compensated metabolic alkalosis and dehydration. The haematocrit will be increased, as will urinary bicarbonate excretion, the latter to compensate for the alkalosis. Potassium will be lost in exchange for H^+ ions, producing hypokalaemia and chloride will be lost with gastric acid (HCl). The pH will rise with the alkalosis.

49 D E
Salpingitis (PID) may be acute or chronic in its presentation. Patients

typically complain of severe bilateral lower abdominal and pelvic pain. Deep dyspareunia is a common and distressing complaint, often requiring surgical clearance of the pelvis in intractable cases. Acute salpingitis may be confused with ectopic pregnancy, as the patient presents with severe pain and the lower abdomen is acutely tender and distended with guarding and rebound tenderness.

50 A B
The term hyperplastic vulval dystrophy or squamous cell hyperplasia is used to describe the vulval condition in women with histological evidence of hyperplasia occurring without a clinically obvious cause. Atypia of the epidermal cells may accompany the hyperplasia and predisposes the skin to malignant change. Symptomatic treatment of the condition includes the use of topical steroids and bland ointments such as calamine cream or zinc and ichthyol. Surgical excision may be necessary to relieve pruritus and prevent malignant change. Paget's disease of the vulva is also called non-squamous vulval intraepithelial neoplasia. Senile dystrophy is also called primary vulval atrophy or kraurosis.

51 A
Dysfunctional uterine bleeding (DUB) is defined as heavy menstrual loss in the absence of identifiable pelvic pathology, pregnancy or general bleeding disorder. Anovulatory DUB is associated with a variable menstrual pattern, the commonest type being prolonged cycles followed by heavy persistent vaginal bleeding. Dilatation and curettage is employed for diagnostic purposes and is rarely therapeutic.

52 A D E
A sterile speculum examination is performed to confirm premature rupture of membranes by visualising a pool of liquor, to obtain a high vaginal swab for infection screening, to assess cervical dilatation and exclude cord prolapse. Digital examination is discouraged to avoid introducing infection. Management is along conservative lines and involves bed rest, tocolysis with beta-sympathomimetics if contractions occur in the absence of infection, and corticosteroids to encourage foetal lung maturity. Caesarean section is indicated only if foetal distress develops, or if there is a foetal malpresentation in labour.

53 B C D E
Occasionally ovarian teratomas may contain active thyroid tissue (struma ovarii) which produces thyroxine, and symptoms of thyrotoxicosis may

develop. Granulosa cell tumours produce oestrogens which produce symptoms that vary with the age of the patient, from precocious puberty to postmenopausal bleeding. Masculinizing tumours such as androblastomas first lead to loss of feminisation with amenorrhoea and breast atrophy followed by virilization i.e. acne, hirsutism, deepening voice and clitoromegaly. Human chorionic gonadotrophin is produced by the germ-cell tumours.

54 A C

In polycystic ovary syndrome the plasma LH levels are increased with FSH remaining low or normal. The LH:FSH ratio is typically >3:1 in this condition. The oestradiol levels are normal but the oestrone levels are chronically elevated due to its increased extraglandular conversion from androstenedione. Ovarian and adrenal testosterone production is increased. Sex hormone binding globulin levels are reduced, resulting in an increase in free testosterone and oestradiol. The typical ultrasound features are enlarged ovaries with numerous subcortical cysts and increased ovarian stroma.

55 A B C D

Ineffective uterine contraction and retraction after childbirth can result in postpartum haemorrhage (PPH). Ineffective uterine action may follow the use of uterine muscle relaxants, e.g. halothane, and when the uterus has been overdistended, e.g. with polyhydramnios. In multiple pregnancy bleeding from the large placental bed and uterine overdistension both play a role in producing the PPH. When the placenta fails to separate completely or if it is retained after separation, the uterus is unable to maintain effective contraction and retraction of the placental site.

56 D E

Breech presentation occurs in 40% of pregnancies at 24 weeks, but by 34 weeks the majority have undergone spontaneous version to a cephalic presentation so that it is seen in only 3% of term pregnancies. It is not a cause of premature labour but is seen more frequently in preterm deliveries because it is more common before 36 weeks. An extended breech is sometimes called a frank breech, and a complete breech is called a flexed breech. In footling presentation the foetal parts fit poorly in the lower segment and prolapse of the cord is a likely complication. Because of the increased foetal risks, vaginal breech delivery is not favoured by many obstetricians especially if associated with any other obstetric problem. If a trial of vaginal delivery is attempted in the remainder the Caesarean section rate in labour approaches 50%.

57 B C D

Bladder papillomas cause haematuria which may be mistaken for post-menopausal bleeding. Endometriosis is a disease of the reproductive age group.

58 B C

Pelvic pain is the commonest symptom of endometriosis and is rarely colicky in nature. It usually occurs premenstrually or with menstruation, but in some women pain is worsened in the days after menstruation. One explanation for the latter is that the ectopic endometrium is less sensitive to ovarian hormones, and shed and bleed later than the uterus. Mittelschmerz is midcycle pain from rupture of the ovulating follicle. Endometriosis only occasionally affects the appendix. It most commonly involves the ovaries and the peritoneum.

59 A B

The age-related risk of developing salpingitis is highest between the ages of 15 and 25, being approximately 1 in 8 to 1 in 10. It is related to sexual activity. The cervical mucous plug prevents ascending infections during pregnancy. Salpingitis occurs commonly after childbirth because this barrier is lost during parturition. *Chlamydia trachomatis* is the commonest affecting organism and accounts for about 50% of cases. *Mycoplasma hominis* causes 10% of infections. Salpingitis is usually a bilateral infection of the tubes.

60 A

Intramural fibroids and submucous fibroids can cause severe menorrhagia, the mechanism of which remains contentious. Various theories proposed include enlarged endometrial surface area, venous congestion and disordered local prostaglandin synthesis. Pressure from an enlarged uterus on the bladder can cause frequency of micturition and some patients may complain of stress incontinence, but this is not characteristic. Rarely, intramural fibroids may mechanically block the cornua resulting in subfertility.

ANSWERS TO PRACTICE EXAM 5

1 A B C D

Seeing coloured haloes around lights is a common symptom in glaucoma.

2 A B E

Complications of acute myocardial infarction include arrhythmias, heart failure and cardiogenic shock, ventricular septal rupture, ventricular wall aneurysm, papillary muscle rupture or dysfunction and pericarditis.

3 A B C E

Ampicillin treatment alters vaginal flora and promotes candidiasis, as does atrophic vaginitis (seen in post-menopausal women) and pregnancy. Immunodeficiency states, resulting in defective T cell immunity, predispose to fungal infections. Immune functions decrease with increasing age. Diabetes is a common predisposing factor.

4 B C E

Aetiological factors in emphysema include smoking, exposure to coal dust and alpha$_1$-antitrypsin deficiency. Patients with long-standing disease may develop a barrel chest. They may be clinically cyanosed and oedematous ('blue bloater') or pink and breathless ('pink puffer').

5 D E

'Acidophil' is an out-dated term for pituitary cells that secrete growth hormone (somatotrophes) and prolactin (lactotrophes). Adenomata are frequently resected using the trans-sphenoidal route. Serious side-effects include CSF leak and meningitis but are uncommon. Acromegaly has been treated with external beam irradiation and pituitary yttrium implantation. All of these treatments can cause hypopituitarism. Prolactin secretion is suppressed by bromocriptine, and the peripheral actions of growth hormone are opposed by somatostatin analogues.

6 A E

Pseudomembranous colitis is treated with metronidazole or vancomycin; the pruritus of cholestasis with cholestyramine and syndrome of inappropriate ADH secretion with demeclocycline. Treatment with amiodarone may result in hypo- or hyperthyroidism. Impotence is a rare complication of treatment with bendrofluazide.

7 A B D
Diarrhoea and pseudomembranous colitis complicate antibiotic therapy, as does vaginal (but not oesophageal) candidiasis. Some broad-spectrum antibiotics cause bone marrow suppression (e.g. chloramphenicol and co-trimoxazole).

8 A B D
Multiple myeloma commonly presents with back pain and vertebral fractures. A spastic paraplegia may result as a consequence. Other features include anaemia, immune paresis, hyperviscosity syndrome, hyper-calcaemia, peripheral neuropathy and amyloidosis.

9 C E
Diabetics in the non-ketotic hyperosmolar state should be rehydrated with isotonic crystalloid; molar solutions are extremely hypertonic. There is no metabolic acidosis so bicarbonate has no role. An intravenous infusion of insulin is used to normalize the blood glucose slowly. Subcutaneous heparin is used as prophylaxis against vascular thrombosis. Common causes of death in these patients include pulmonary and cerebral oedema. Antibiotics should be considered, as infection is often the precipitating cause.

10 A B C D E
Sputum production in bronchiectasis can be extremely copious and may be blood-stained. Characteristically there is an obstructive deficit on lung function testing. Patients with chronic suppurative lung disease are usually clubbed and are at increased risk of developing cerebral abscess. This disease can be complicated by amyloidosis.

11 B D E
A homonymous hemianopia is caused by unilateral lesions in the optic pathway proximal to the optic chiasm. Involvement of the optic tract causes an associated acuity loss as the macula is involved, but in lesions of the optic radiation the macula is spared. Pituitary tumour results in a bitemporal hemianopia as it involves the optic chiasm. Retrobulbar neuritis will result in scotomata or complete blindness.

12 A B C D E
Atypical or neurotic depression can present with agitation, poor sleep with waking late, mood worse late in the day and increase in appetite. More commonly, depression is associated with decreased activity, reduced appetite, poor sleep with early awakening, weight loss, poor concentration

and decreased facial expression. Hallucinations may occur in patients with psychotic depression.

13 A B C D E

A myelopathy caused by an intradural, extramedullary mass can present insidiously or suddenly (typically after a fall). Therefore a meningioma compressing the spinal cord can present not only with a gradual onset of vibration and joint position sense loss with areflexia below the level of the lesion, but also with an acute paraplegia with sphincter involvement. In lesions presenting acutely there may be a flaccid paralysis. In chronic or late lesions, there is usually a spastic paraparesis.

14 B

In mixed mitral valve disease, signs of dominant incompetence include a displaced, diffuse apex beat, soft first heart sound, pan-systolic murmur and third heart sound. Left atrial dilatation and pulmonary hypertension are features of mitral stenosis and incompetence.

15 B D

Meningiomas in the olfactory groove and demyelinating plaques may directly affect the optic nerve and result in unilateral blindness. Lesions of the optic tract and occipital lobe may cause a homonymous hemianopia. Lesions of the optic chiasm result in a bitemporal hemianopia.

16 B C D

A pseudobulbar palsy is caused by bilateral upper motor neurone lesions of the ninth to the twelfth cranial nerves. The tongue is spastic and the speech 'hot potato'. The jaw jerk is brisk. Associated findings include dementia with emotional lability and a shuffling gait the 'marche a petit pas'. Inhalation pneumonia is a common complication due to weakness of the bulbar muscles. The commonest cause of pseudobulbar palsy is atherosclerosis resulting in ischaemia affecting both cerebral hemispheres.

17 A B

Ulcerative colitis is a disease in which inflammation is limited to the mucosal layer of the colon. The rectum is always involved and proximal involvement is variable but always continuous. Crohn's disease causes a trans-mural inflammation that can affect any region of the gastro-intestinal tract, not necessarily in continuity. The incidence of carcinoma of the bowel is 3–5% in both and the incidence of cholelithiasis is not increased in either.

18 A B C E

Except for myotonic dystrophy, myopathies affect the proximal muscles first, and distal weakness is usually due to a peripheral motor polyneuropathy. The myopathy induced by alcohol is usually proximal, but any muscle group can be involved. The vinca alkaloids are neurotoxic and may cause muscle weakness and pain. Pyramidal weakness is caused by cerebral hemisphere lesions. Proximal and distal muscles are involved, with weakness of the upper limb flexors and the lower limb extensors.

19 A B E

Causes of malabsorption are divided into dysfunction of the pancreas, the biliary tree, the small bowel lumen or the small bowel wall. Neomycin-induced malabsorption is multifactorial. It binds bile acids, alters the luminal flora and affects mucosal function.

20 B C

Lymphocytosis is seen in infections, such as those caused by viruses, particularly infectious mononucleosis, *Toxoplasma* and *Bordatella pertussis*. It is also seen in malignant disorders of lymphoid cell lines (the lymphatic leukaemias). Systemic lupus erythematosus causes a lymphopenia and leptospirosis causes a neutrophilia. Whole body irradiation causes bone marrow suppression and a cosequent lymphopenia.

21 B D E

Lupus is suspected in patients with polyarthralgia, Raynaud's phenomenon, photosensitive skin rash, alopecia, mouth ulcers, a peripheral blood lymphopenia/thrombocytopenia, and serositis (pleurisy/pericarditis). Laboratory corroboration includes raised ESR with normal or raised C-reactive protein (CRP), circulating anti-nuclear antibodies with DNA-binding specificity, false-positive syphilis serology and depletion of complement factors.

22 A D E

Septal defects do not cause congenital cyanosis, but increased blood flow through the pulmonary vasculature leads to pulmonary hypertension and raised right heart pressure. The direction of flow through the defect may then reverse and cyanosis appears. This is called the Eisenmenger phenomenon and tends to occur in large defects, more commonly in VSDs than ASDs. This may also occur as a complication of patent ductus arteriosus.

23 A D E

Chlamydia trachomatis infection is the most common cause of blindness: five to ten million people are blind because of trachoma. It is transmitted from eye to eye by flies, fomites and fingers. Early infection is cured with topical tetracycline.

24 A B C E

Foxes and dogs eat sheep offal contaminated with *Echinococcus granulosum*. Hydatid disease occurs in humans when vegetables or water contaminated with the faeces of foxes or dogs is consumed. Hydatid cysts can develop in any structure of the human body, usually the lung or liver.

25 B C D

Rheumatoid arthritis is characterized by a symmetrical polyarthralgia affecting the metacarpophalangeal and proximal interphalangeal joints. The joints are stiff first thing in the morning but fatigue later in the day is typical. Examination of affected joints reveals tenderness and boggy synovial swelling. Onset can occur at any age but most frequently presents between the ages of 35 and 45. Females are affected three times more frequently than males.

26 A B C D E

Generalized wasting of the small muscles of the hands is a feature of motor neurone disease, syringomyelia and as part of the cachexia seen with bronchial carcinoma. Neurogenic wasting of the hand muscles is seen in lower motor neurone lesions of T1 nerve root or the ulnar nerve. It is also seen secondary to disuse in rheumatoid arthritis. Wasting of the thenar muscles may be seen in carpal tunnel syndrome. Involvement of the upper limbs usually occurs as a late feature of Friedreich's ataxia.

27 A B D E

Indications for excision or diagnostic biopsy of pigmented lesions to exclude malignancy include change in colour or size, bleeding, itching and tenderness. The development of shades of red, white or blue within a previously uniform pigmented lesion might indicate malignant change. Excision should also be considered in lesions that are raised, with an irregular border or irregular surface. Malignant change from a mole is very rare in children.

28 A

The onset of Parkinson's disease is usually between 55 and 70 and a positive family history is rare. The increase in tone is extrapyramidal, not pyramidal, and ankle clonus would suggest a Parkinsonian syndrome rather than idiopathic Parkinson's disease. The tremor may be increased by chlorpromazine.

29 A D E

The facial nerve is the seventh cranial nerve. It supplies motor innervation to the facial musculature except for masseter, temporalis and the pterygoids (the muscles of mastication) which are supplied by the fifth (trigeminal) nerve. It also supplies taste sensation to the anterior two-thirds of the tongue, autonomic innervation to the lacrimal glands and the nerve to stapedius. It divides into its five terminal branches within the parotid gland. Malignant tumours of the parotid gland may involve the facial nerve.

30 A B C

Adrenaline, glucagon and growth hormone all increase blood glucose; adrenaline acts to increase hepatic glucose output, and glucagon also increases hepatic glycogenolysis. Aldosterone has principally mineralo-corticoid activity. Sulphonyl derivatives stimulate secretion of insulin and hence produce a fall in blood glucose.

31 B C D

Factors predisposing to the development of the respiratory distress syndrome are those that delay the maturation of surfactant. Maternal toxaemia and heroin addiction accelerate surfactant formation and thus 'protect' against this syndrome in the newborn.

32 B C E

Nerve damage may require explorative treatment as may acute compartment syndrome. Healing occurs more quickly in children than in adults – hence bones unite in about 3 to 4 weeks.

33 C D

The metaphyses are more commonly affected in children, with *Staphylococcus* being the most common pathogen. Parental treatment is required to avoid the development of chronic osteomyelitis. X-rays are very unhelpful in making the diagnosis and the ESR is usually raised.

34 E

The boundaries of the triangle are the medial border of adductor longus, inguinal ligament and medial border of sartorius. The lacunar ligament is a reflection of the inguinal ligament at its inferior medial portion. The lacunar ligament is the medial boundary of the femoral canal. The femoral vein, artery and nerve all lie within this triangle, but the nerve is not within the sheath.

35 A D E
Inguinal hernia is the most common type of groin hernia in both men and women. Femoral hernia is more common in women than men but is less common than inguinal hernia. Indirect hernia is more common in young men. Bladder is well recognized as part of the contents of femoral and inguinal herniae. Groin herniae are commonly repaired under local anaesthesia (>80% in the USA).

36 All false
Buerger's disease (thromboangiitis obliterans) is (almost) exclusively a disease of young male smokers. It is characterized by occlusive disease of small and medium sized arteries, and superficial and deep veins, and by the occurrence of Raynaud's phenomenon. It is rarely amenable to reconstructive surgery.

37 B C E
The sex incidence of Hashimoto's thyroiditis (diffuse goitrous autoimmune thyroiditis) is 4F:1M. It classically occurs between the ages of 30 and 50 and may cause dysphagia requiring surgery. Hypothyroidism is usually a later development. Thyroid antibodies (antithyroglobulin and antimicrosomal) are usually but not always present.

38 A D E
Decubitus ulcers often develop in seriously ill or debilitated patients nursed in bed. The common sites include bony prominences (e.g. malleoli) and the heel. Varicose veins are not a common cause of cutaneous ('varicose') ulcers which much more commonly are the result of venous hypertension secondary to deep venous incompetence. Compression bandaging will heal many venous ulcers but will exacerbate (often disastrously) arterial ulcers. Rest pain is a common accompaniment of arterial ulcers.

39 A B E
A strangulated hernia contains part of a viscus which is becoming ischaemic. It will be tense and tender. Resonance will not be elicited because the ischaemic organ will usually contain extravasated fluid. An expansile cough impulse is only found when there is movement of the

contents through the neck on coughing. That cannot occur in a strangulated hernia. The greater omentum is often found in a strangulated hernia, particularly in umbilical and femoral herniae.

40 B C E
Peptic ulceration can occur at any site where the bowel is exposed to gastric acid including the jejunum (e.g. in a gastrojejunostomy). Neuropathic ulcers are common on the feet of diabetics who often have associated arterial disease and a tendency to infection. Leg ulcers can also be seen in Felty's syndrome of rheumatoid arthritis, hypersplenism and leucopenia. Rodent ulcers (basal cell carcinoma or BCC) commonly occur on the face, but can occur on the leg and trunk (superficial erythematous BCC). Those on the temple and preauricular areas behave aggressively and may develop invasive squamous cell carcinoma.

41 A C D E
Distension of the gallbladder occurs in patients with obstructive jaundice without gallbladder disease (i.e. without gallstones); hence Courvoisier's Law which states that a patient with obstructive jaundice and a palpable distended gallbladder does not have gallstones. Carcinoma of the ampulla of Vater will produce obstructive jaundice with a distended gallbladder in up to 50% of cases, and carcinoma of the head of the pancreas in up to 30% of cases. Carcinoma of the duodenum is very rare but may also produce obstructive jaundice due to obstruction of the common bile duct. Cholangiocarcinoma of the common bile duct may produce a distended gallbladder; however a tumour of the hepatic ducts will prevent bile entering the cystic duct.

42 B
Tuberculous lymphadenitis may produce a 'cold abscess' when several tubercles coalesce to form a single lesion; which will lack the inflammatory features of a pyogenic lymphadenitis but which may produce an abscess which will fluctuate. 'Rubbery' nodes are characteristic of lymphoma including Hodgkin's disease. A pharyngeal pouch bulges posteriorly between cricopharyngeus and the inferior constrictor muscles of the pharynx and then projects laterally usually on the *left* producing a diffuse swelling of the neck. Pulsatile swellings in the neck (even if thought to be transmitted) should always be referred for a specialist opinion as they may be a carotid aneurysm or a carotid body tumour both of which require specialist facilities for their safe treatment. Branchial cysts should be treated surgically as they may become repeatedly infected making subsequent surgical treatment more difficult.

43 A D E
The parotid is most commonly involved in a neoplastic process although about 85% of parotid tumours are benign. Although the proportion of malignant tumours is higher in the other salivary glands, parotid carcinoma is more common overall. The facial nerve is commonly involved in malignant parotid neoplasms whereas it is very rarely involved in benign neoplasms. Although ulceration into the mouth or through the overlying skin is unusual, it may occur. Carcinoma of the salivary glands is a disease of the elderly; and the prognosis is generally poor.

44 C E
Acute otitis media is usually unilateral and commonly affects children. Infection is thought to enter via the Eustachian tube from the oropharynx. The mastoid air cells are only rarely involved. Barotrauma more commonly causes chronic nonsuppurative otitis media but may cause acute otitis media.

45 C E
Scalp lacerations are usually simply sutured. They are commonly associated with an underlying skull fracture and are thus technically compound. They require antibiotics but not usually surgery. Fractures over the sagittal sinus are usually not operated on unless causing pressure symptoms as they can bleed torrentially when explored. However, depressed fractures over the motor cortex commonly cause convulsions and so should be elevated. CSF rhinorrhoea lasting for longer than 10 days suggests a fracture involving the frontal or ethmoid sinus and should be explored because of the risk of aerocoele or meningitis.

46 A C D
Simple closure is the treatment of choice (combined with peritoneal lavage) and further definitive surgery is not usually (<25%) required subsequently. Gastric outlet obstruction requires bypass (e.g. gastrojejunostomy) or occasionally a pyloroplasty. Misdiagnosis may lead to delayed treatment of a colonic perforation or of biliary disease, but if the patient is not settling on conservative treatment surgery should be performed. Ramstedt's procedure is performed for infantile hypertrophic pyloric stenosis.

47 A C
Tenesmus or a painful desire to defaecate (often without success) is characteristic of low rectal tumours. Fissure *in ano* causes exquisite pain after defaecation. Haemorrhoids and fistulae are usually not painful

unless complicated by thrombosis or abscess respectively. Pilonidal sinus is remote from the anus (in the natal cleft) and will not cause pain associated with defaecation.

48   C D

Erb's palsy is the result of a birth injury or of falls or blows on the shoulder, producing forcible separation of the head and shoulder. It results from an upper brachial plexus injury (mostly the C5 root). The arm is held internally rotated and the forearm is pronated. There may be sensory loss over the outer arm. The prognosis is usually good and the arm is held in an abduction splint with a moveable elbow joint. However if recovery does not occur arthrodesis of the shoulder joint may stabilise the arm and forearm for controlled distal movement. There is no relation (other than nominal; they were both described by the same physician) with Erb's syphilitic spinal paralysis, a form of progressive spinal paraplegia.

49   D E

Hypertension, albuminuria and oedema constitute the triad of signs characteristic of pre-eclampsia. Hydatidiform mole may be associated with very early and severe pre-eclampsia.

50   A C D

Open neural tube defects and multiple pregnancy are associated with abnormally high levels of alpha-fetoprotein in the liquor amnii. High serum AFP alone indicates an increased risk of obstetric problems in later pregnancy including intrauterine growth retardation (IUGR) and perinatal death.

51   A C D

Uterine rupture and inversion of the uterus can cause profound postpartum shock associated with variable amounts of vaginal bleeding. Paravaginal haematomas may be large enough to cause shock with little or no associated vaginal bleeding and should be suspected in cases of unexplained postpartum shock, particularly after instrumental delivery. Intravenous ergometrine is used to control postpartum haemorrhage, a common cause of obstetric shock. Third degree tears may occasionally produce postpartum shock associated with excessive bleeding.

52   C D E

Hyperemesis gravidarum or excessive pregnancy vomiting is a feature of twin pregnancies and is associated with hydatidiform moles. It is attributed to high circulating chorionic gonadotrophins, and not pituitary gonadotrophins. The condition is believed to have a psychosomatic element, hence the beneficial response noted when the patient is removed from her usual environment and admitted to hospital. Gross prolonged hyperemesis may result in various degrees of disturbed liver function.

53 A C D E

Low grade cervical dysplasia presents as mild dyskaryosis in cervical smears. Infections such as trichomoniasis and candidiasis are associated with inflammatory smears. The cervical smear pattern in normal pregnancy usually resembles that seen in the normal secretory phase. Rarely, there may be some clumping of cells due to an exaggerated progesterone response in pregnancy, rendering the smear unsuitable for diagnosis. Occasionally, decidual and Arias-Stella changes may be mistaken for dyskaryosis.

54 A C E

The conditions for a forceps delivery are that the foetal head is fully engaged and that the cervix must be fully dilated. The membranes should be ruptured and the position of the head should be known before forceps are applied. The bladder must be empty.

55 A C D

Migraine headaches, depression and loss of libido have all been associated with combined contraceptive pills. Other adverse associations include breast enlargement, bloating with fluid retention and weight gain, cramps and pains in the legs, nausea, vaginal discharge and break-through bleeding.

56 A B C E

The first phase of the menstrual cycle 'the follicular phase' is characterized by the development of follicles. The progesterone concentration and hence the body temperature is lower than in the luteal phase of the cycle. Proliferation of the endometrium occurs in the second half of the cycle and so the endometrium is relatively thinner on day 7. A cervical smear on day 7 gives a characteristic fern-like appearance.

57 B C E

Trichomonas vaginalis is a protozoan and it is a common cause of vaginitis. It is often associated with pruritus and a yellow, purulent and odorous discharge which may be frothy. Metronidazole is the drug of choice.

58 D E

Peripheral resistance decreases by 40%, plasma renin activity increases at least five times and cardiac output increases by 30%. Aldosterone excretion increases at least four times and the pre-ejection period is significantly reduced in the first two trimesters.

59 A D E

The glomerular filtration rate increases by 60%, urate excretion by 40% and folate excretion is 3–4 times the non-pregnant level. Glycosuria is common in otherwise normal pregnancy partly due to less efficient glucose reabsorption by the nephron. Ureteric dilatation is probably obstructive in origin rather than due to muscular atony.

60 C D

In uncomplicated pregnancies there is no evidence that hospital admission confers any benefit. Delivery before 38 weeks greatly increases the risk of neonatal respiratory distress syndrome and if it can be delayed to 39 weeks the outlook is much improved. Purified insulin is less likely to evoke antibody formation, hence the risk of foetal cell damage is reduced. Urinary glucose measurement is unreliable in assessing diabetic control but it gives a measure of the rate of dietary carbohydrate loss.

This is a list of recommended books that you may like to buy, borrow from a library or share with friends.

MEDICINE

D C Sprigings and J B Chambers, **Acute Medicine**, Blackwell Scientific Publications, 1990.

D Rubenstein and D Wayne, **Lecture Notes on Clinical Medicine**, 4th ed., Blackwell Scientific Publications, 1991.

P Armstrong and M L Wastie, **Diagnostic Imaging**, 3rd ed., Blackwell Scientific Publications, 1994.

R Robinson and R B Stott, **Medical Emergencies – Diagnosis and Management**, 5th ed., Butterworth Heinemann, 1987.

Procedures in Practice, 2nd ed., The British Medical Association, 1988.

P J Kumar and M L Clark, **Clinical Medicine**, 2nd ed., Ballière Tindall, 1990.

R A Hope and J M Longmore, **Oxford Handbook of Clinical Medicine**, Oxford University Press, 1986.

J A B Collier, J M Longmore and T J Hodgetts, **Oxford Handbook of Clinical Specialties**, 3rd ed., Oxford University Press, 1992.

J R Hampton, **ECGs Made Easy**, 2nd ed., Churchill Livingstone, 1992.

J R Hampton, **ECGs In Practice**, 2nd ed., Churchill Livingstone, 1992.

A Haddad and D C Dean, **Interpreting ECGs**, 2nd ed., Blackwell Scientific Publications, 1987.

GENERAL SURGERY

H Ellis and R Calne, **Lecture Notes on General Surgery**, 7th ed., Blackwell Scientific Publications, 1987.

P G Bevan and I A Donovan, **Handbook of General Surgery**, Blackwell Scientific Publications, 1992.

139

ORTHOPAEDICS

R M Kirk, **Clinical Surgery in General**, Churchill Livingstone, 1993.

P S H Browne, **Basic Facts of Fractures**, 2nd ed., Blackwell Scientific Publications, 1988.

R McRae, **Clinical Orthopaedic Examination**, 3rd ed., Churchill Livingstone, 1993.

A G Apley and L Solomon, **Concise System of Orthopaedics and Fractures**, 2nd ed., Butterworth Heinemann, 1994.

T Duckworth, **Lecture Notes on Orthopaedics and Fractures**, 3rd ed., Blackwell Scientific Publications, 1995.

OBSTETRICS AND GYNAECOLOGY

G Chamberlain and J Malvern, **Lecture Notes on Gynaecology**, 7th ed., Blackwell Scientific Publications, 1995.

G Chamberlain, M Pearce and P Hamilton, **Lecture Notes on Obstetrics**, 6th ed., Blackwell Scientific Publications, 1992.

A W F Miller and R Callander, **Gynaecology Illustrated**, 4th ed., Churchill Livingstone, 1993. (Also available as an International Student Edition.)

PAEDIATRICS

D Hull and D I Johnston, **Essential Paediatrics**, 3rd ed., Churchill Livingstone, 1993. (Also available as an International Student Edition.)

SLIDES AND PICTURE TESTS

M Parsons, **A Colour Atlas of Clinical Neurology**, 2nd ed., Wolfe Publications, 1992.

M Zatouroff, **Physical Signs in General Medicine**, Wolfe Publications, 1984.

W F Walker, **Diagnostic Picture Tests in General Surgery**, Wolfe Publications, 1987.

V R Tindall, **A Colour Atlas of Clinical Gynaecology**, Wolfe Publications, 1988.

V R Tindall, **Diagnostic Picture Tests in Obstetrics and Gynaecology**, Wolfe Publications, 1987.

G S J Chessell, M J Jamieson, R A Morton, J C Petrie and H M A Towler, **Diagnostic Picture Tests in Clinical Medicine – Volumes 1, 2, 3 and 4**, Wolfe Publications, 1984.

INDEX

Index

Index

PASTEST BOOKS FOR PLAB CANDIDATES

PLAB Practice Exams: Medical Sections
Contains 240 MCQs, four Clinical Problem Solving exams, and tips on the Projected Material exam and on the viva.

PLAB Practice Exams: English with Tape
English for the PLAB Test with Tape
Each book contains English Comprehension Tests (with tapes) plus written English test papers, sample essays and letters, and advice on the oral.

Postgraduate Medical Training in the UK:
A Guide for Non-UK Qualified Doctors
Information on the National Health Service, the General Medical Council, British postgraduate medical exams and on living and working in Britain.

PasTest have over 22 years' experience of helping doctors to pass postgraduate examinations. Used together, our revision books and intensive courses provide the practice you need to succeed. Contact PasTest at the address below for more details and a current price list.

PASTEST INTENSIVE PLAB REVISION COURSES

Our week-long PLAB revision courses run three times each year at a convenient central London venue. The course includes multiple choice questions, clinical problem solving papers and slide sessions. The optional intensive English teaching sessions include spoken and written tests.

✓ Skilled Tutors - learn from Consultants and Senior Registrars with extensive teaching experience

✓ Pre-Course Exam - assess your strengths and weaknesses and identify areas that need attention

✓ Past Exam Questions - used throughout to ensure you become thoroughly familiar with all aspects of the exam

✓ Examination Technique - develop successful methods to deliver "model" answers and achieve high marks

✓ After Course Preparation - tips and suggestions to assist you with your personal last minute revision plans

For full details and to reserve your place contact PasTest today:

PasTest, Dept. PM, Egerton Court, Parkgate Estate, Knutsford,
Cheshire WA16 8DX
Telephone 01565 755226   Fax 01565 650264